Dethroning Sacred Spaces

The Hidden Truths of How to Reduce Stress and Burnout, Increase Productivity and Achieve Wholeness at Work

Dr. Frances Yahia

Contents

Introduction

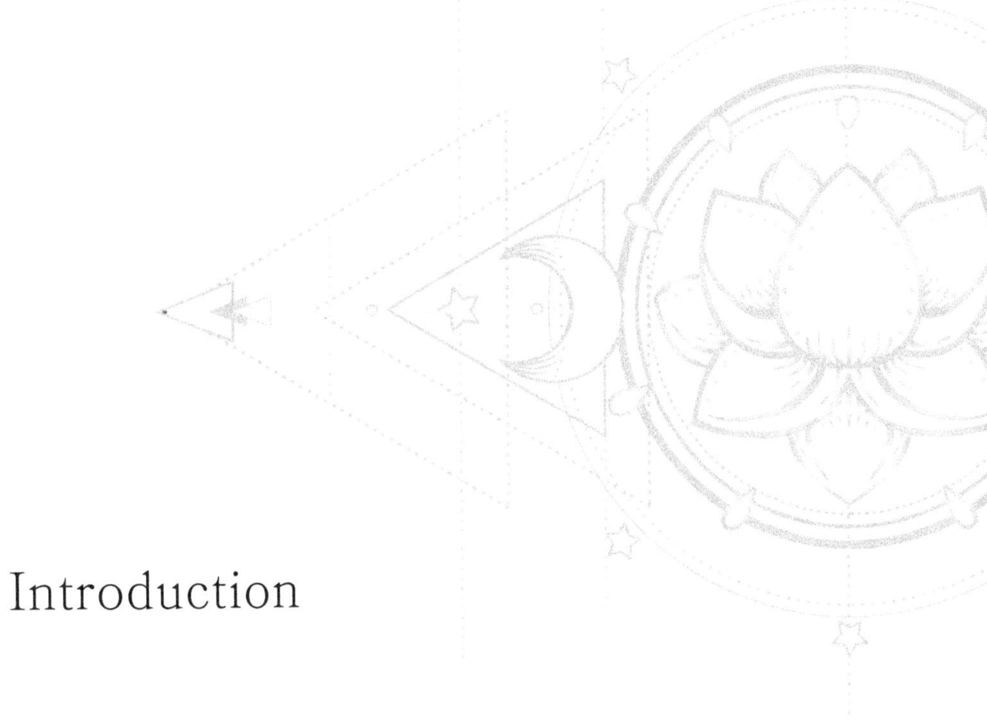

The subconscious mind doesn't shut down just because you go to work—you bring yourself with you. Your unmet needs, your value system, your low-level consciousness and your childhood programming—that's all dragged with you to your job. To think that it's not would be silly. That's what we're going to deconstruct in this book.

This book is about dethroning sacred spaces because we don't oftentimes think that work is a sacred space, but it's where we spend most of our time. It would be kind of a strange perspective to think that it's not sacred or that we can't do spiritual or mental health work in the environment where we spend most of our time. Yet we don't tend to think of work as a sacred space.

There are always two levels of consciousness working in our lives: an earthly consciousness, which includes awareness of our body, our surroundings, others, what we would call the material world; however, the behind-the-scenes consciousness few people tend to be connected to as easily is the spiritual consciousness, and it is equally as important. Unified consciousness is when the earthly world and the universal consciousness act in tandem and support one another so you can achieve wholeness, contentment and happiness. We think it is isolated to certain events, for instance, thinking of someone and the phone ringing and it's them on the other side of the phone. But this consciousness is working in us, around us and for us all the time.

I invite you to flow between both levels of consciousness as you read this book and work these themes in your life. Think of it as dual citizenship of two countries, and the metaphysical law called the *Principle of Correspondence*, which I'll describe in depth, is the passport to help navigate both levels of consciousness. The purpose of this book is to engage both levels of consciousness in the work environment, where on average we spend most of our waking hours, thereby, making it a space that meets our earthly needs, like our financial and professional needs, yet, can also meet our spiritual needs as well.

The workplace is the most sacred space, teaching us that the material world serves and supports the spiritual focus of our lives. In this book, I reiterate concepts from my previous books, including *The Seven Gates: Seven Steps Beyond Self-Awareness*, where I explain that the subconscious stores everything that then leads us to who we are, where we work, and what we can or cannot achieve. Without identifying your subconscious patterns and limiting beliefs, you cannot live a whole life, but rather, will live the unlived lives of your parents, thinking it is yours, and never begin, much less complete, the hero's journey.

Four Stages of Subconscious Development

The subconscious is developed at the moment of conception, where we get our entire programming for a lifetime. This is the first stage of subconscious development. At that moment, we choose our parents based on a vibration, and this determines our level of consciousness. The purpose of a lifetime is to raise that consciousness level; however, the only way to do so is with others mirroring our flaws back to us. I will discuss archetypes and shadow aspects of people you work with, and whom you may judge, while they are really representing aspects of yourself you're unable to see as you learn to understand what you're really judging is yourself. These are called unintegrated aspects of your psyche, or shadow aspects, that we get from our parents at conception.

The second stage in the development of the subconscious is pregnancy. Our pregnancy was a toxic, parasitic environment where our mother taught us a shadow love language. This language keeps us in child mode, seeking our needs via manipulative means. We learn to put on the mask required of us, to simply get a conditional version of love. Our work relationships and environment mirror the unhealthy womb space we occupied for nine months.

Working through the issues at work, as it reflects the womb, is often how we rebirth ourselves into wholeness.

During birth, our third stage of the subconscious is developed. The birth process is how we transition through life, from job to job or position to position. We mirror our exact birth story in these professional transitions. Transitions are pushes into unchartered territory, liminal spaces that afford us opportunities to identify our own value system and find a personal truth.

Lastly, the early years from zero to seven give us the earthly story we will attach to in our rational consciousness that keeps us living a life of inherited limitations, but most of all keeps us only honoring our human existence without paying much attention to our spiritual consciousness. During the zero to seven years, our inner child developed when we were shamed and believed we were not enough. During zero to seven we developed our ego, personality and persona, and our soul took a backseat. During these years we also chose, subconsciously, our preferred archetype, which aligns with the mask we tend to wear at work.

My hope is that through this raising of consciousness around your shadow aspects that colleagues and superiors are modeling to you, you can reclaim your soul and divine will and purpose to individuate and live a full life of workplace wellness and eudaemonia, meaning contentment and wholeness. I introduce my "Chocolate Chip Theory of Leadership," which is a metaphor I use to explain our universal consciousness, earthly consciousness, and how everyone at work is a chocolate chip (an archetype), mirroring you back to yourself.

All of my teachings are rooted in Universal Law, eight universal truths that are found in any tradition and philosophy and can be applied to any environment. I'll be focusing on the Principle of Mentalism, Principle of Correspondence, Principle of Rhythm and the Principle of Cause and Effect in this book; however, all eight laws are found in my book *Hidden Truths: The Magic of Mysticism and Its Modern-Day Applications Eight Universal Laws of the Universe and How They Can Work for You*. The universe is not literal; that is why the earthly consciousness is not sufficient to grow, change and be whole and healthy. In *Hidden Truths*, I also lay out the twelve truths to a spiritual path, which follows the *Labors of Hercules* and our life path as we mature physically and spiritually.

Eight Universal Laws of the Universe

- Principle of Mentalism
- Principle of Correspondence
- Principle of Vibration
- Principle of Polarity
- Principle of Rhythm
- Principle of Cause & Effect
- Principle of Gender
- Law of Octaves

The eight universal laws dictating all of life's cycles listed in Hidden Truths: The Magic of Mysticism and Its Modern-Day Applications Eight Universal Laws of the Universe and How They Can Work for You

The universe speaks in symbol, myth, metaphor and archetypes. The archetype guiding this book is the archetype of Saturn or Cronus, named after the Roman and Greek god of sowing, wealth, and plenty because he reigned the Golden Age of plenty. Under Saturn's rule, humans enjoyed the spontaneous bounty of earth because he represented both Greek words for time, *kairos* and *chronus*: right timing and chronological time. Using the metaphor and myth of Saturn teaches us that the chronological time we spend at work, punching the timeclock, if used appropriately, as right timing, we can grow both our earthly and spiritual bank accounts.

The book also discusses how your work family resembles your childhood family, where now as a physical adult you can choose to heal childhood wounds, through the archetypes you encounter in your work life, again unifying your earthly story and your spiritual awareness to raise consciousness.

CHAPTER 1

Universal Law, Mythology & Archetypes

Spiritual growth is programmed into our DNA, just like physical growth is. You're going to age. Do you want to age gracefully? If so, you probably watch your diet, exercise, and stress levels. You are guaranteed a certain amount of spiritual growth by virtue of being a spiritual being, however, with knowledge of universal laws, and by using these laws during work hours you can grow exponentially.

Raising consciousness and transmuting limiting childhood beliefs inherited at conception is a process—not a linear one, not a short one; it's lifelong. Our spirituality, and our search for it, is inherent in our thoughts, in our day-to-day actions, in cycles we go through in life. If you can understand this, you can understand that we are never divorced from our spirituality because spirit is who we truly are, and why all spaces are sacred spaces.

Universal Laws

The first universal law is the Principle of Mentalism, and it states that the ALL is mind and the universe is mental. What you think will create your reality. This is the spiritual law that, whether we know it or not, we are held to. The concept of ALL is mind refers to one overarching mind of the universe where nothing is dual; however, in the spiritual aspirant (occupying the earthly realm), our reality is dualistic in nature. At conception, you inherited a mind, and from that inherited template you will create everything else in your life, and it will be created from that low vibration unless you transmute those limiting beliefs and create from a higher vibration. As your subconscious mind changes, your earthly life changes—this is the Principle of Mentalism.

The main universal law I'd like to introduce in this book is the Principle of Correspondence, which is reflected in this ancient maxim: "As above, so below; as within, so without." This principle embodies the truth that there is always a correspondence between the laws and phenomena of the various planes of being and real life as we live it every day. Everything you experience in your earthly world is a mirror of what is happening inside, mainly inside your head. Your entire life, and the mind you're creating it with, rooted in the Principle of Mentalism, is mirrored back to you in every earthly interaction. All conflicts are created by your mind to show you where you need to integrate aspects of your psyche that were inherited at conception and modeled as a fragmented self, during childhood. In spirituality, there is no other, so everything is created by your mind for you to grow and learn. For instance, If I judge my physical environment is disastrous, it's indicating that my inner environment is disastrous, too.

Indeed, Matthew 6:10 (NIV) states: "Your kingdom come, your will be done, on earth as it is in heaven." This verse relates to the Law of Correspondence. With its application, the universe speaks to us moment by moment. In my first book The Seven Gates, I speak about 'milking the moment'. Milking the Moment is a strategy I use with clients to teach them the Law of Correspondence. When I teach this, I tell students to pay attention to sensations in their body—what they hear, feel, smell, taste, and what is going on externally—while they're asking the Universe for internal guidance. We can only experience the Divine through the form and the senses, heightened awareness let's us identify how the Principle of Correspondence is working through us. Later in the text I'll refer to the functions of illness. Often illness is a divine way to to bring us back into the form, to unify consciousness.

The next law, the Principle of Rhythm, states, "Everything flows out and in. Everything has its tides. All things rise and fall. The pendulum swings, manifesting everything. The measure of the swing to the right is the measure of the swing to the left. Rhythm compensates." Life has a rhythm. This law refers to that rhythm. We see this rhythm in, for instance, the tides four times per day, the moon cycles every twenty-nine days, the four seasons each year, and the planets orbiting in the solar system. The rhythm of life is circular, and the point of tension of that circle is called an opposition; the pendulum will swing from right to left, from one extreme to the other. Saturn cycles are thirty years long, yet every seven years, what I call skinny cow years, you will have a point of tension and a crisis. These years are part of our earthly chronological time, to slow us down and recalibrate to what is important. Saturn teaches us to bend, be humble, reevaluate and plant seeds at the appropriate time for future growth cycles. During Saturn (or skinny cow cycles) my clients will use words like stuck and have a sense of falling behind, when really, they're recalibrating. Kairos or divine time catches up once the new vibration and consciousness has anchored into the psyche. I use the mystical symbol of the enneagram, a metaphysical symbol that dictates all of our cycles; however, I have adapted it to help you calculate your role at work and the cycles in your professional career throughout your life. I will offer calculations for you to calculate your work number, at your current position, or anywhere you become employed. This number will correlate with your inner child and childhood wounds meant to be worked through in that role. Although the enneagram is not original, the calculations linked to your work number and inner child is original to this book.

The Principle of Cause and Effect states, "Every cause has its effect. Every effect has its cause. Everything happens according to law. Chance is but a name for law not recognized. There are many planes of causation, but nothing escapes the law. Nothing happens by accident." *Everything happens for a reason.* I dislike that statement for its overuse, but it's true. In essence, that's what this law is about. There is a law that governs what's happening. You may not know the law, but whatever is being mirrored to you is indicative of what the law is trying to demonstrate. Accept your limitations, but know that there is a reason for the reason. You created the karma because of your past deeds. You're not privy to that information, but the universal law states that you're not in your current life situation by accident.

Ralph Waldo Emerson said the Law of Cause and Effect is the "law of laws." All actions have reactions. What you initiate has consequences and will return back to its point of origin. All paths have an origin story and from that a chain reaction of events occurs. What determines the effects of your actions? It's all linked back to consciousness. If you enter into a behavior with conscious action, you will get that in return. Unconsciousness around a situation that you initiated does not keep you from the consequences of what you initiated.

When you were conceived, the level of consciousness at which you were conceived started a chain reaction for the next nine months of your mother's pregnancy and then on into your lifetime. Everything in your lifetime is a result of that one moment in time when you inherited your conception story. As you grow and gain consciousness, you can change the result of what happens as a result of your actions, if you change your level of consciousness. However, you can never change the origin story that began at the moment of conception. This is the thread of your lifetime. You're the product of desire. This poses so many issues within, because it is desire, we are invited to eradicate in order to be considered spiritual and worthy; however, desire is fire, passion and creation and what motivates us to grow and change. It is understanding how the desire we are rooted on, through our conception, serves to propel us forward, yet, mirrors what needs acceptance in oneself. The meeting of this consciousness within is often understood through the years we spend at work. We spend 90% of our fire trying to change the unchangeable in our nature, simply because we have believed our conception based on desire is unworthy. I will go into the concepts of transcendental and tribal narcissism later in the book and how we use pain or pleasure as our preferred version of desire; to punish ourselves for our desirous moment of conception. Wholeness is achieved when these aspects of ourselves are integrated, what I describe as dethroning the COO, being original and ordinary.

The myth of Odysseus in Homer's *Odyssey* is a perfect representation of the importance of our conception. Odysseus is gone to war for ten years, and as a result it takes him ten years to return home. When he encounters his wife twenty years later, they're in the marital bedroom rearranging furniture, and he says, "You cannot separate the olive branch from the marital bed." The bedpost was made from the olive branch that was coming out of the floor. This illustrates the point that everyone is a product of their parents, good and bad, and you cannot remove your parents and their influence from your story or your psyche. Therefore, their level of consciousness is dictating all of your future behaviors, hence, the results of your life when you live from an unconscious state and take no responsibility for anything—until you decide to change. The workplace is often the best space to encounter ghosts from the past from conception through childhood and work through the issues to become the higher consciousness version of yourself and midpoint of your parents, indeed the olive branch. I'll discuss how your work family resembles your childhood family as a means to work through wounds of perfection, criticisms, validation and judgment.

Saturn or Chronos Archetype

Saturn is represented by this symbol that looks like a sickle and cross. Saturn is the cross that we bear, and most people would say that their work is a cross, a burden. In mythology, Saturn was dethroned by his son. Saturn is the archetype of authority—boundaries, the king, stability—that gives us limits. Usually we don't like these limits. This is related to our childhood and to our yearning to escape work. Astrology is tied to these myths and to the bigger picture of why we work.

The glyph of Saturn. It represents the cross we bear.

"He was dethroned!"—the word *dethrone* has a sense of competition. What do most people want? They want to climb the ladder of success. They don't like the CEO, authority, or boss. I had a client say, "I don't like my boss! She is wicked." What we judge is what we are. Judgments are confessions, and they're great.

I responded to her, "That is why you are in this relationship, because that boss is mirroring you."

There's a sense of hierarchy or of climbing the ladder because Saturn was dethroned. Saturn rules the workplace, limits, ambition, and the paycheck. Saturn is also known as Chronos, and rules the time clock that we're all watching. Saturn represents the archetype of grief, melancholy, depression, limits, and boundaries. At the psyche level, Saturn is known as the karmic taskmaster. When you are conceived, you are metaphorically castrated because the universal consciousness that you are and come from, is limited to a body, a karmic pattern for this lifetime and a low level of consciousness riddled with limiting beliefs. In mythology Uranus, the sky god, represents our unlimited potential and the Universe within each of us; but Saturn castrated Uranus, his father. He castrates us with a body, limits, boundaries, money, and earthly responsibilities. The minute that we are conceived, The Fates, in particular Clotho begins to weave your fate or destiny. It is tied into every story, relationship and job. It cannot be escaped. Saturn, gives us our karma. He says, "Here's your karma for this lifetime, this is what you came to do." To believe there is a spiritual space dedicated to growth attempts to separate your life's purpose from day-to-day living. Accessing temples, ruins or retreats may give you a respite from your daily life, that may appear to not be spiritual or sacred; however, what Saturn emphasizes is the daily grind (your job and your body) as the true temple where your life plays out and leads to transmuting limiting beliefs and raising consciousness.

You are burning karma at work. You're working through your karma with the people that you are helping. You learn flexibility, boundaries, and limits. There is a path of yoga called karma yoga, and it simply means *action*. Go pull the weeds and help with service. I always say, "The purpose of life is to learn how to die." This is all the domain of Saturn. The place this happens, day in and day out, is at work. Do not think that you're not at work for some really cosmic reason.

CHAPTER 2

Workspaces as Sacred Spaces

Your work is your most sacred space; your work is your most spiritual space. As a spiritual student, you learn to say, think, and do. You speak up for yourself, you voice what you want. It's a place where you learn humility, a big spiritual lesson. You think that we must leave our nine-to-five work life to do spiritual work. We must dethrone sacred spaces. You're not leaving your job to go to a sacred church or temple on the weekend that's more sacred than your job. My hope is to bring you back to what's called trial and denial: Saturn. Because we keep doing the same day repeatedly.

The most spiritual movie is *Groundhog Day*. Every day, he does the same day repeatedly. That's why work is called the daily grind. The same thing: the same teachers, the same meanings, the same people, the same lunch hour, the biggest life-changing lessons. You're here in a workspace to get tried, to get out of denial.

Johnathan was a client who kept switching jobs every two years. He repeatedly encountered the same type of boss, someone who didn't appreciate him or value his efforts. After four job changes, when he came to work with me, he started understanding that his supervisors were representative of his own lack of self-worth. He had judged himself for never finishing graduate school, so he subconsciously devalued himself because he didn't have the credentials he deemed valuable. Once identifying the subconscious patterns and his limiting beliefs, he was content at his current job and eventually got promoted.

One of the things that Saturn does is it leads us to grief. Grief is when we use something until it no longer is purposeful. Saturn's life cycle is thirty years long. We identify adulthood at thirty years old. We are productive for thirty years. Our mortgage is thirty years. These cycles represent a Universal Law called the Law of Rhythm, stating everything has a season and everything is cyclical. We assume adulthood at thirty, with kids, mortgage, marriage, and around sixty we finish paying it off, retire, have grandkids. Obviously these cycles are changing, but this is the traditional cycle and it's all dictated by Saturn. This is part of our daily life, our earthly world language; it's not separate from spirit. There's a reason those are your years where you deconstruct your values and meet your spiritual family.

Your work environment is so supremely important to teach you humility and other spiritual lessons. Realize what you value a lot of times is the need for validation. You need your boss to stroke your ego. You need a paycheck to say you're worthy. All the things you learn when you retire and dedicate yourself to your spirit. The ashram tradition sets a framework. Often when people retire, they give back through volunteering, or they have a life review and go to therapy if widowed, etc., so in these ways the spiritual life takes on a greater focus than the material. Don't waste thirty years of productivity and work. Your work can be your spiritual teacher, meeting mind and matter at its finest.

Saturn is also teaching you that you misuse your resources. Time, money, and resources—in other words, energy—is your currency of self-worth. Saturn is here to teach you through a job, authority, a schedule, and money that you're using your resources incorrectly. Through Saturn's wisdom of trial and error you will learn self-love. Once you value your time, money and resources, limitations and structure no longer feel restricting, rather safe. Saturn teaches us to feel safe within ourselves. There are four unmet needs from childhood, safety, security, validation and love. Nobody's childhood was safe, because it lacked clear transparency; therefore, the trial and error of speaking up, what feels right, how to spend your time and respect your money and resources, is the way to understand Saturn's lessons. The 30 year Saturn cycle teaches you what is simply knowledge in your head, to become wisdom in your heart.

Saturn is also known as Chronos, which means time. Chronos holds us accountable to time. It slows us down or bends us to be flexible. It's the cross we all bear, and the reason is we must soften our rigidity. We've got to soften the "truth" we think we have. All truths are half-truths. We must become more supple and tolerant. As the karmic taskmaster, Saturn teaches us that our truth is not a truth, but rather an opinion. As we bend and become more tolerant, we can see life through another's vantage point. This leads us to release resentments and forgiveness within. At conception, since it was rooted in desire, there is an inherent belief that we are unworthy and worthy of rejection and abandonment. This leads us to take things personally and believe anyone that sees things differently is against us. It's a defense mechanism to feel a sense of love and belonging. Though Saturn's teachings and use of the Principle of Correspondence, ultimately you realize that everyone is a mirror to your own subconscious beliefs around your own failings as a desirous being. As we mold to understanding others, the wounds from childhood don't own us any longer, rather we provide fertile soil for another to grow from our story. Saturn was the god of the harvest and had fruitful crops, year in and year out, for this reason.

The body part that Saturn rules is your knees. It brings you to your knees! How often are you humbled or humiliated at work? Things in life that bring you to your knees will teach you humility—to bend, to soften, to be supple, to be flexible. There's no better sacred space than our work environment. Humility is the name of the game.

Saturn is the only planet that makes us *refined*. I'm using this word intentionally. From an archetypal perspective, Saturn is snobby, ambitious, focusing on quality not quantity. He teaches us that our innate resources are enough. Simplicity is not simple. It teaches us to be simple, refined, detached, yet value our destiny and gifts that entered with us at conception. Capricorn is the sign that's ruled by Saturn. The goat that rules Capricorn only eats the good fruit at the tippy top of the tree. The part of you that's snobby, that wants the Prada purse and the fancy restaurants, is your archetype of Saturn. Climbing the ladder of success is what gives you self-worth. What refines us in spirituality is to realize you are worthy independent of those things. Alchemy is a branch of spirituality. Alchemy is taking lead, a heavy brick, and refining it into gold. That's why you work, that's why you're in the same environment day in and day out. It is your refinement process.

Saturn or Chronos also rules old age and the sage archetype. At ages zero to seven, you have your origin story; this sets you up for life. The struggles of childhood, where you had no agency, set up your work life pattern. You'll re-enter the childhood snowglobe, as I call it, and confront those struggles, but now having a voice and agency over your choices. At fourteen, you attempt to find your own value system. This begins our spiritual infrastructure, defining our own values and philosophy of life. The workplace offers opportunities for self-betrayal and walking one's authentic path by fighting for your values, an agency you did not have at 14. At twenty-one you identify your sexual pleasures or financial strategies. There's an independence found with sex and money and you try different things on for size. The full Saturn return at 28 is a modified castration where you oblige to societal norms of adulthood that may feel like shackles until you work through the archetypes of freedom and limitations, a common theme found in our work life. These are all Saturn cycles. We need lived experience, and that is why Saturn is our most beloved teacher. In the myth of Phaeton, the son of Helios the sun god, Helios has horses that carry a chariot that takes the sun across the sky every day. Phaeton discovers that his father is Helios. Helios promises Phaeton one wish, anything he wants. Phaeton asks to drive the chariot that carries the sun in the sky every day. Helios refuses because he knows Phaeton is too young and can't control the horses. His son begged him and despite knowing it was not the thing to do, he gave in. Helios gave him the reigns of the chariot, knowing he wouldn't have the capacity to take the sun across the sky. Phaeton crashes the chariot into earth and sets the earth on fire. Part of the work experience is learning our limits. In childhood, we are often too limited, or like Phaeton, given too much power without knowing how to use it. Time and our work lives teach us the give and take of how to handle power or when to relinquish it.

A lot of times, people are turned down for promotions because they don't have enough experience even though they could do the job. Lived experience is a parcel of our spiritual growth. Phaeton crashes the sun and the chariot into the earth, causing the big fire. Sometimes—we need to crash and burn until we realize we must do something differently. Saturn aims to teach us that there is a different way to do things; it bends it, makes us supple and teaches us humility. The Law of Rhythm and another metaphysical law the Law of Polarity speaks to the pendulum swings in behavior change. We swing from extreme to extreme, and with Saturn cycles, and trial and error, we slow the swings and gain self-mastery. Oftentimes in our work environment, we meet the mentors and sages that teach us how to slow these swings, but we also meet the nemeses that force us to take risks and leave the status quo, even if we crash and burn a time or two.

To be a spiritual student is to own your power. You can't get there at twelve; you can't get there at fourteen. You're just not enough yet, or you don't know that you're enough. From the moment of conception, you're always enough, but you haven't had enough lived experience. As you get older, and with Saturn's help, your rigidity softens you up and makes you the brilliant sun that you are. This process takes some time. The problem is competition. We think things are competitive. We think that we can lose and win. You can win and lose in your earthly world in your body. You cannot win in your spiritual life, there's no winning or end point.

There's no better place to learn to work and play than work. It's part of why tribal societies did it all in one. You need to go slow, on Saturn time. Chronos slows you down. If your fire is too strong; if you don't contain yourself, you burn everything up like Phaeton. If you're too afraid to ask, because you were shut down, you won't take risks or use your fire appropriately, but rather be fearful. Oftentimes, illness is just a manifestation of how strong or weak your fire is. We will discuss the functions of illness in Chapter Four. Fire is the only element humans have control over. It is linked to conflict and chaos when not contained properly and passion, desire and creation when used correctly. We need authority, limits, and boundaries so that we can slowly develop the fire. We need age, time, and years; that's the limitation that's in the psyche reflected by Saturn and his wisdom. You don't want to be contained, so we need authority, limits, and boundaries so that we can slowly develop the fire. We need age, time, and years; that's the limitation that's in the psyche.

There's a false belief that freedom is having no boss or timeclock; however, in the name of that freedom many blow up their life. Freedom is a state of mind. Freedom is only achieved when impure thoughts and limiting beliefs about our desires from conception are processed and allowed room to breathe. It is Saturn that softens the chains throughout his cycles inviting you to look at the rigidity of your false beliefs, the ones that make you feel castrated and chained. You're obligated to earthly time, but why not make it count while you're here? It will be years before you can become the perfect ripe fruit on the tree. The Law of Rhythm states there is a season for everything and primarily speaks to the Saturn cycles that appear every seven years. Age is needed to grow spiritually; that's why I call the Saturn years the skinny cow years. Skinny cows are on schedule every seven years, from birth to death. They enter your life to help you refine yourself, detach from outdated limiting thoughts and help you become the sun god (Helios with the correct strength to drive the chariot) that you are here to become. The concept of the skinny cows comes from the

Bible story where Pharoah dreams of fat cows being eaten by skinny cows. Joseph prophesizes that the years of plenty will be followed by years of scarcity. We follow this same cycle for our soul's growth. If we, like Pharoah, do inner work during the abundant or fat cow years, the skinny cow years will be less stressful, but either way, the skinny cows help us to slow down, re-evaluate our thoughts and what is important and grow. The fat cows follow because the expansion from releasing ourselves of limiting thoughts is true freedom. Without tension from a boss, colleagues, a limitation, it is impossible for us to question what is no longer working and seek the soul's purpose; therefore, rather than blowing up your life in the name of freedom, release pressure from the castrating thoughts by seeking further into what the supposed limitation is trying to teach you.

Saturn rules thirty years of financial productivity, feeling limited, and answering to something or someone. Around sixty we long for retirement, endless golf courses and generative activities; however, your spirituality isn't put on hold until 60+. It is in your day-to-day. The holy is in the day-to-day. Your work and your relationship with your boss, colleagues and peers is your holy, sacred space.

In childhood no ones needs were met entirely, especially safety needs We all grew up confused! One reason we feel limited at work is because there is clarity. It seems counterintuitive that we would run from safety, clarity and transparency, but the psyche associates lack of clarity, boundaries and pain as love. At work there are clear guidelines and a handbook. You understand the consequences of your actions; therefore, your psyche feels uncomfortable without the guesswork. In Chapter 7 I will go into detail about how our work family resembles our childhood family. Since no family was 100% clear on expectations when the workplace hold's us accountable it feels like the opposite of family and our dysfunctional version of love. As the subconscious developed in the womb, we also received a false definition of love. Whatever negative feelings mother experienced during pregnancy is how we interpreted love to feel. In my book *The Shadow Side of the Mother's Love* I explain that eliminating that negative feeling is akin to death so we try and avoid it all costs and rather invite the negative feelings. When things are clear, like at work, our negative feelings aren't warranted so to speak because we know the consequences. What happens is we tend to find work environments that mirror the same issues as our childhood family so we can attach negative feelings and love to our work experience. Learning to confront these aspects of ourselves, speak up, ask for limits and boundaries becomes scary because we are in essence confronting our "gods" (parents) in the guise of a boss or co-worker. Since our biggest fear is lack of love and belonging, growing in a work space forces us to choose ourselves and finally discover that love is not pain and love and belonging is found within. If there is clarity around rules and expectations, the only thing that is safe and clear from day one is your job. Here's your handbook, here's your manual. These are the rules! You come in late, you get written up. You call out sick, you don't get paid. Clarity. Yet we say that work isn't sacred or spiritual? However, It's the most sacred space. Work is the most sacred space because it gives you boundaries, limits, rules, and structure. And you get paid! Can spirit or matter ever be separated? No. The other reason we don't like work is because it forces us to adult. When you start, you are given a rulebook! Nowhere else in your life do you get the opportunity to adult. You adult through your bosses, your authority figures, your paycheck, your schedule, and the time clock. At work, we have very clearly spelled-out expectations. At home, we didn't; therefore, the safety and clarity of work for most of us is uncomfortable because we are seeking mother and father in every place and space. We don't like to adult. Clarity feels restrictive. Anywhere there is clarity, there's authority and removes the ability to stay in victim. The place we are most loved is where our needs are met. The place we are most loved is where we have rules. Your day-to-day is your discipleship.

Liminal means threshold and refers to a space in transition. When we go to work, we're in a transition space, and there's an opportunity to do our spiritual work, to look at our mind, our thoughts, our judgments. It's material in nature because it's associated with the clock. It's where we spend most of our week and how we earn money. It actually is the most liminal space. You cannot grow your money or grow your spirit without a limitation or a container. Our tendency is gluttonous, but without a limitation or a container like the workplace, we would self-destruct like Phaeton.

Zelos, this is the god of competition. The word zealous comes from the Greek god Zelos, and it means to advance and compete with others at work. In the Roman pantheon, it's equivalent to the god Invidia. Envidia is the Spanish word for jealousy and envy. What do you envy at work? Do you envy those who make more money, have higher positions? You might envy someone who is out sick for the day or has more vacation time than you.

The workplace is the most sacred space because you're getting confronted with the thieves of your mind at all times. Work is a liminal space. Liminality is the space between; it's a threshold or a transition space, the overlap between work and the sacred. In the past, in order to enter a spiritual tradition, you would get initiated. Initiations invite ceremony and ritual, to anchor in the mysteries.

The liminal is the transition between states of being and is ruled by Saturn. Your years of hard work, that you view as separate from your spiritual life, are the transition years to get you ready for what the Vedas call Moksha, the liberation for your spirit. In the Vedas, ancient Hindu texts, at sixty, you'd retire from earthly life and move into the ashram and work on your spirit; however, we don't need to wait, we can do this work within the day-to-day. We think it's reserved for the church, the mosque, the ashram, or a vacation when we go on a sacred retreat. We think it's reserved for when we're older; it's not. It's the day-to-day where you get polished.

Work provides a liminal space, a space of transition on your way to becoming your true self or divine being.

Thin places are known as sacred spaces, where one can walk in two worlds; according to which thin places give meaning to the moments in life. Thin places are places of energy, where the veil between the material and the ethereal is thin. It's where heaven is no longer so far from you in the present moment. You can obtain so much of the universal goodness that the space between the vastness of the universe and this earth becomes thin. If you've ever gone to a church or a sacred site, this will make sense.

I went on a sacred pilgrimage many years ago to Lourdes and Fatima. These are very marked, spiritual, thin places. There's something palpable where you feel God's presence; or whatever you deem God to be. People have gone there so often, lit candles, incense, prayed, got water and brought gifts. You feel it: it's thin. It's like there's no difference between spirit and matter in those spaces. The form and formless become one. This is the essence of spirituality.

Have you ever gotten to your job before anyone else, where the lights are out and it's kind of dark? That's a liminal space. A thin space. In architecture and in decorative terms, it's known as liminality, or liminal spaces. *The New Yorker* states liminal spaces are in-between places that exist as a means to an end, to be traveled through, but not lingered in. Liminal spaces are a metaphor for God, the breath and transition periods similar to adolescence. The breath is what connects us all. It reconnects to us to ourselves to pause and make a choice that supports our values. Work, similar to adolescence, is a liminal space where we learn life's lessons but our time there is temporary. Through these transitions spaces, as we take a pause and breathe, and make life choices, we discover the god within and encounter the god in others mirroring ourselves back o ourselves. Work years mold you from a child into a spiritual adult via the Saturn or senex archetype.

Your office is a thin place. Understand the opportunity that you're having through that conversation with that boss, supervisor or colleague is a space where breath and the divine, resides. All of a sudden, you're not hating the grind. Liminal spaces are absence of light and the absence of people. You don't see exactly who you are just yet. Again, this is where the magic lives; taking a situation and shifting perspective about what it offers. The liminal space of work is directly linked to who you are becoming.

A ***temenos*** in Greek is a piece of land cut off and assigned as holy precinct for a sanctuary, holy grove, or holy precinct. Think of it as an ashram land, a sacred land, or a piece of land. Jung called the therapeutic space, temenos. Jungian psychologists see the process of individuation as taking place within a liminal space. Since individuation requires the breakdown of a persona, it's a liminal space, as they rebuild themselves and make themselves whole again. Carl Jung considered psychotherapy and the therapeutic relationship to occur in a liminal space or a container, a temenos or magic circle (derived from the Greek's word) because the client's transformation would take place in this space.

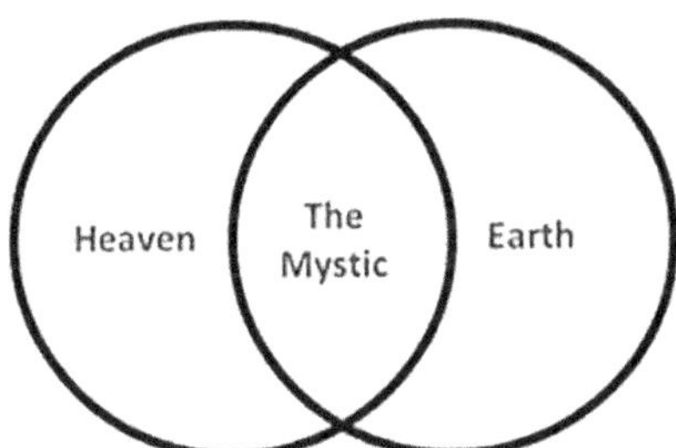

The Vesica Pisces, a sacred geometry symbol of two overlapping circles, represents that spirit and matter or heaven and earth always meet. The overlapping space is called a mandorla, and the liminal space where as humans both earthly and spiritual consciousness reside. The mandorla, where the shaman or mystic lives, is a metaphor for using both states of consciousness, spiritual and material, in all spaces. This space is also the temenos, the therapeutic space, Jung referred to as the container for healing.

Vesica Pisces is a symbol in sacred geometry. The overlap of the circles is a mandorla and is where the spirit and material meet. It's a liminal space where we live when we are living in wholeness and is what we can achieve at work if we consider work a sacred space. This is the space in therapy where the therapist and the client meet and find that intersection of spirit and matter, or individuation.

Work is the opportunity that we have, the temenos, the container to unravel and piece ourselves back together again, whole. We see this teaching in varied spiritual texts and traditions. In Ayurveda, you eat for the seasons, so in the winter and fall, you eat colors of golds and reds. Think of squash, pumpkin, and pomegranates. Then in the spring, you eat more bitter foods like watercress and celery. If you eat for the seasons, according to the *Caraka Samhita*, the main Ayurvedic text, you're considered healthy. There is a liminal space in between each season called *ritusandhi*. Studies show that seasonal changes create greater imbalance in your physical and mental health. According to the Law of Polarity we swing during these transition spaces o balance out and achieve self-mastery. Work like the seasons is a liminal space, a swing of the pendulum back and forth to achieve self-mastery. Buddha walked around with a bowl, begging. Buddha could not reach enlightenment without nourishment; he had to eat food to sustain the matter. He denied his body of food and grew weak and skeletal. Finally, he realized this self-mortification was going to kill him. Sujata, the daughter of a local villager, brought him a bowl of sweetened rice cooked in condensed milk. Eating the rice, feeding the body and engaging in pleasures led to his enlightenment. In Buddhism, every monk receives a bowl when they're initiated and they carry it with them wherever they go. They accept what is offered. The bowl is a reminder that in order to serve the spirit, the vessel of the body must be cared for. The bowl represents the Middle Way: avoiding extreme practices and extreme attachments. Work, our paycheck, learning what we value in terms of material possessions, ambition and how to manage our time and resources is the equivalent of the Buddha bowl. Neither seeking only sweet rice or none at all, leads to enlightenment or self-mastery. Work provides the linimal space to nourish our material and spiritual needs adequately.

The first stage on a spiritual path is truth of thought, and a basic tenet in spirituality is that there is no 'other'. If I understand that each thought I have had about another has created the world I live in and is a reflection of myself, then every space can become sacred space. That's the beauty of the intersection of work as a sacred space. I no longer must see it as the other, the boss, the authority, the castrating timeclock, or the limited paycheck; it's about me. It's all me, that's where we use work for our growth advantage. One of the things that happens during *ritusandhi* is that your hair and nails become dry. The dryness of the seasons causes brittle hair and nails. The thing that is used in Ayurveda to balance the dryness is oil, what is known as *sneha*, the Sanskrit word for oil and love. You can go to work and become dry and bitter for thirty years. At the end of those years, you will get dry and bitter. The shadow side of the sage or senex, is bitterness, melancholic, critical and dogmatic. Oil is symbolic of love. You need flexibility, you need suppleness, you need to bend; when your boss tells you something you get humble, get on your knees. Don't be so rigid, no one's doing anything to you; you're doing it to yourself. It's with that suppleness, with that sneha, that love, hopefully you will learn to love yourself despite your shortcomings; that will keep you from being dry and bitter. In between the liminal spaces, in between the spirit and the matter, in between the seasons, in between the thirty years that Saturn mandates you perform the daily grind, you are being molded by the sacred space and liminal space of work, to cultivate self-worth and self-love.

We become very dry and brittle, like our nails during the winter. You know that sound when the wind breaks the ends of your hair. This is very important symbology; you've got to grease the wheels. You've got to soften up. If not, Saturn will beat you down until you learn the lesson. That's the entire purpose of karma; that's the whole purpose of the Law of Cause and Effect. That's the importance of the seasons and the Law of Rhythm.

One of the things I love about the workspace are the rituals. In our work day, we should find time for ceremony and ritual, which balances the work life. Play is what fuels creativity, so to be more productive, breaks are necessary. Morning coffee, breakroom cafecito, lunch dates or Monday morning football—these are rituals that we maintain at work. There's some real beautification in work, in the sense of the ritual of getting together with people all the time. Being productive, yet, engaging in those rituals is part of the way we play while at work. Every single day, we are provided time to engage in those rituals. If we consider that, we can really use work as a sacred space.

When people state that they're sick to death of working, or that they got sick from stress, they're buying into work as sickness, and blaming authority, structure, and limits instead of owning that they're in the exact place they need to be by culture, by vibration, by energy. Because we chose that place to learn spiritual lessons.

British anthropologist, Victor Turner states "we now separate work as if it's not holy. The fading of liminal stages in exchange for liminoid experiences is marked by the shift in culture from tribal and agrarian to modern and industrial." Where we used to be agriculturally based, everybody did everything on the land, or with the tribe; that moved to more of this modern industrial society. This has somewhat created the separation between work and spirit, if you will, in these societies. Turner stresses that "work and play are now entirely separate, whereas in more archaic societies they're nearly indistinguishable. In the past, play was interwoven with the nature of work as symbolic gestures, and rights to promote fertility, abundance, and the passage of certain liminal phases. Thus, work and play are inseparable and often dependent on social right." It used to be interwoven; there wasn't any difference between spirituality and materiality. Now we're very segregated, and we're missing a thirty-year-plus opportunity to grow spiritually. Saturn is saying use the sacred space, use the workspace, use these productive years to be spiritually productive, as much as materially productive. The liminal space is of spirit and matter, but now we see it as a space that beats us down, that makes us sick. We're so stressed out and burned out. We're not taking the essence of the spiritual teaching from work, thinking that it's separate.

Gallup states that nearly 70 percent of employees are actively disengaged, a Harvard Business Review survey reveals; 58 percent of people don't trust their own boss, and more than half of U.S. workers are unhappy in their jobs. Let's shift the perspective that we cannot grow spiritually, mentally, and emotionally at work. A bodhisattva is the representation of Buddha on earth. A disciple uses the world—aka, the rice bowl, the job, the limits, the boundaries—to feed themselves spiritually and materially. Use the temple that is work, the sacred space that is your work life to become the bodhisattva.

CHAPTER 3
Dethroning Limitations

Dharma is a concept from Indian philosophy and although it is not precisely translatable, dharma is the concept of limitations and expansion. We often have the idea that if we are limited, it castrates our expansion, but it's the opposite. The dharma wheel, one of the eight auspicious symbols in Buddhism includes the teachings of Buddha to control the mind: right mindfulness, right view, right intention, right speech, right action, right livelihood, right effort, and right concentration. In Patanjali's yoga sutras, they're the yamas and niyamas.; moral codes or right living. Unless we understand what we're thinking wrongly about, we can't achieve right mind. By dethroning perceived limitations, like the workplace, we break the belief that structure and limitation doesn't allow for expansion, but rather embrace the concept that through limitation we expand. Authority and limits allow for spiritual and material growth, rather than the belief that they limit our opportunities. Thich Nhat Hanh said, "Every thought you produce, anything you say, any action you do, it bears your signature."

The metaphysical Law of Correspondence states "as within, so without". This implies that anything manifested in your external world is a representation of your internal world. Since the workspace is where we spend most of our day, use of this law during work could help us grow financially and spiritually. Understanding that those limitations we feel externally coming from work—

authority figures, colleagues, frustrations—when we use them in the context of this law, as a mirror, can help us shift inwards and grow spiritually.

Archetype of Time and Cycles

In mythology Saturn, or Cronus, is father time and represents the sage or senex archetype; however, his shadow side is rigidity and feeling limited. It had been prophesized that he would be castrated by his son; therefore, Saturn would swallow his children for fear of being dethroned and losing his reign. A shared human experience is feeling castrated, because at the moment of conception we were given limiting thoughts. We project these limitations on those that we feel limit us; however, it is only giving our limiting thoughts some breathing room where we find growth and expansion. Time, also linked to Saturn, devours us. If we waste our limited time on earth not only aging physically, but becoming a sage, we are missing the point. In the New Age, the concept of transcendence has taken on an implication as if it occurs outside of the realm of time or outside of the body; however, transcendence cannot occur without the earth, the form, limits and a body. We can only change and transmute within the form. Saturn makes us feel as if we are against the clock; however, *kairos*, divine time, makes time feel as if it stretches to accommodate the transcendence. If we "consciously corporate" by using the workspace to grow inwardly, we can meet Saturn's demands, yet transcend the mental limitations imposed on us from conception.

*Image of the oil painting **Saturn Devouring His Son**, by Spanish painter Francisco Goya created between 1819-1823 and housed in Museo Nacional del Prado.*

In Vedic mythology the god Indra represents limits and order. It is believed that the form is the only thing that holds the disorder or chaos. In Greek mythology, the Titan goddess Themis is believed to rule our low-level consciousness animal nature, often associated with desires, the flawed form and the impure body. This erroneous belief is why we feel separate from the divine. It is only through what is known in Sanskrit, an *ishta-devata*, a god as form, that we can know the divine as humans in an earthly form. The misconception that the transcendent is out of the form or viewed as perfect keeps us from fully embracing ourselves, lower nature and all, and others and their lower consciousness, fully. In analytical psychologist's Carl Jung's book, *Answer to Job*, he states that humans change God. Since God can only be experienced through the body and senses, learning to see how our colleagues, coworkers and bosses can help change us, is the most divine experience. We need form to hold all things spiritual, we need limitations to have a transcendent experience. Transcendence only happens within what we consider to be limits.

When we start off in our work life, we are not seasoned. This is why Saturn swallows us in terms of time. Jung's archetype of *puer* and *puella* is used to describe an adult whose emotional life has remained at an adolescent level. The work life, the workspace, those years of work are a useful opportunity for you to get seasoned, day in and day out, and to realize that you are the source of unconditional love. The Peter Pan archetype is an example of a puer, the one that never wants to grow up. The puer/puella is not an issue in the early years, because this is age appropriate. We expect an eight- or nine-year-old child to be childlike. It's when we are older, in that adult environment, that it really becomes a problem, and we have to grow out of this stage. It's work, boundaries, limitations, budget, paycheck, authority or the CEO, that really helps refine us. Puers often have a hard time with commitment. Think of when you first started your work life and its commitment; you probably didn't want to clock in every day. You didn't want to be there all the time. Maybe you lied and said you were sick. Most of us go through that seasoning period. We like to keep our options open and can't bear to be tied down. This is the idea that freedom is opposite of restriction. We like to keep our options open and can't bear to be tied down. This is the idea that freedom is somewhat outside of restriction.

We can use this seasoning in work life to grow out of such behaviors. Puers often act spontaneously with little thought of consequences. Puers scoff at boundaries and limits. They tend to view any restriction as intolerable. They do not realize that some restrictions are indispensable for growth. The puer has an opposite. All archetypes have an opposite, which we call the shadow. The puer's is the *senex*. The senex is usually what we get as we work and as we get older: someone who is more disciplined, conscientious, and organized.

The I Ching is an ancient manual of Chinese divination based on 64 hexagrams, each interpreted to impart wisdom. It is one of the oldest Chinese classics. It is one of the oldest Chinese classics. The readings linked to each hexagram are elegant, simple and yet, profound. Hexagram number 60, *Jie*, is linked to hesitation, limitations, and discipline. Unlimited possibilities are not suited to man; if they existed, his life would only dissolve in the boundless.

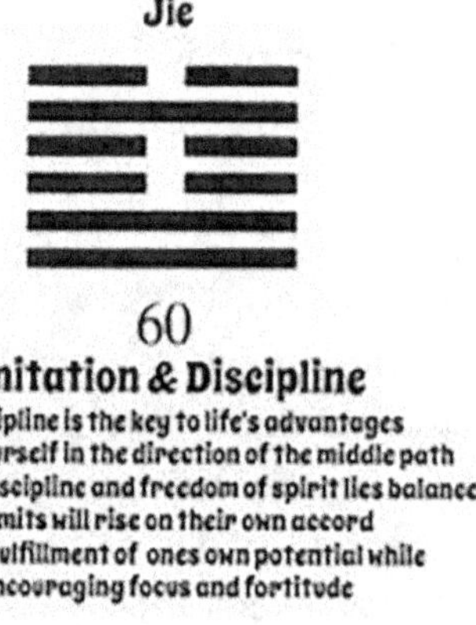

The I ching hexagram Jie, number 60, means limitation and discipline. Limits are necessary to give direction to life.

You cannot have unlimited opportunities or be unlimited without boundaries. To become strong, a man's life needs limitations ordained by duty and voluntarily accepted. It is important that you get there *voluntarily,* not that you are forced there. Consider the transmutation in the mind from a behavior of clocking in everyday, or doing the dishes. In Mircea Eliade's book, The Sacred and the Profane, the author observes that while contemporary people believe their world is entirely profane or secular, they still at times find themselves connected unconsciously to the memory of something sacred. Eliade considered the axis mundi to be the midpoint where the sacred and profane meet. The axis mundi or world axis is the line or stem through the earth's center connecting its surface to the underworld and the heavens and around which the universe revolves. Work provides this midpoint. Ideally, you would consciously transmute your belief system and identify that the sacred is being channeled through you in your workspace; however, through Saturn's seasoning transmutation of your limited beliefs begin to change. Some fight the changes, other bend and fold much easier; however, the sacred will make us yield is some form.

Unus Mundus

Unus Mundus is the Latin term meaning 'one world'. Within the cosmos or the divine consciousness, matter exists, the one world occupies both states of consciousness. The two states of being: spirit and matter. The *Unus Mundus* implies that we occupy both realities at once, neither can be independent from the other.

The Zen koan around enlightenment states, "Chop wood, carry water, get enlightened, chop wood, carry water." The person doesn't look any different because enlightenment, like transcendence, is an internal process. Matter in the form of a body, a bank account or a 9-5 schedule isn't limiting you, enlightenment creates mental freedom from these false beliefs and although everything externally may be the same, everything has changed internally. Ultimately it is through the limitations of your life, that the expansion of enlightenment happens.

Archetypes are mental and energetic forms that we associate with certain qualities and patterns in a person. Since archetypes are energetic patterns, we need the form to identify what they are, if not they'd remain in the ether. Every story from life is channeled through your preferred archetype. There are twelve archetypes that we will discuss later in the book, and every archetype has a shadow aspect. Saturn cycles often force us to encounter our preferred archetype and its shadow. Since these archetypes need to be materialized, it's often in the form of conflict at work we can most easily see them. There's an archetypal theme that weaves your entire life together. Different people and different situations will repeatedly show up to help you integrate the shadow and shift the perspective around the archetype. Different people and different situations will repeatedly show up to help you integrate the shadow and shift the perspective around the archetype.

I have struggled with the concept of leadership and authority since I was a child. Leadership is one of my core values; however, having grown up in a cult, I was determined to not become that type of leader. As I lived out my Saturn cycles, I was learning to master my sage archetype and started finding my groove in the leadership positions that always seemed to find me. I started trusting my inner authority figure. I had repeatedly considered myself a fraud and imposter, not deserving of leadership positions. Until I learned where I was an authority, versus those areas where I wasn't, I hadn't fully integrated the archetype. I had to learn to bend; I had to be flexible. Where is your sage archetype having difficulty shining through because you may fear your inner authority or be rigid in your views? These are the shadow aspects of the sage and they're mirrored to us if we pay attention. Work is filled with restriction and restrictive language. There's a version of a limitation we must endure in the workspace as our inner sage and authority develops. Work teaches you boundaries and provides a container so that our divine will has the opportunity to best be expressed. Change the earthly concept of limitations and restrictions as jarring to the spiritual concept that limitations provide your divine expansion.

In the movie *Groundhog Day*, Bill Murray's character yells, "I'm not the God, I'm a god." His repeat of the same day is akin to the repeat of the skinny cow cycles we endure every seven years with Saturn as we enter the refinement process. We need limitations to get to this point of realization. We are allowed to express ourselves in this world without taking anybody else's power. Here we own our inner authority. Indra, the Vedic god, holds our inner chaos until we can manage ourselves. Since Saturn is archetype that rules alchemy, the concept of taking lead and turning it into gold, through the limitations and container Saturn provides, you're refining your inner chaos to reach the realization that you are a God.

Work teaches you where you need to surrender. It's different for everyone. Maybe your inner authority is about taking charge and speaking up in a meeting, while for another it's about silence and not speaking up. Through our dharma we conform to our duty and our nature. We aren't judging it, but rather surrendering into it. It's been described as a right way of living and a path of rightness, but we cannot learn our dharma, or accept our own nature, without observing ourselves through these Saturn cycles.

Lawrence Kohlberg's proposed three levels of moral development, The first is pre-conventional morality linked to punishment and reward. The second, conventional morality, is linked to good and bad girl/boy behavior; however, his third stage of moral reasoning is post-conventional morality, and is characterized by an individuals' understanding of universal ethical principles. This stage doesn't violate your own values or another's because they honor universal principles, despite our individual differences. Dharma involves acting ethically within yourself, not because it looks good or keeps you from getting in trouble or getting recognition.

This is not something that you just know, this is something you grow into. The law is not spiritual law if spirit and matter, the Unus Mundus, can be separated. Your divine and earthly matter cannot be separated. You're always observing the spiritual law, that's why all spaces are liminal spaces, sacred spaces, or thin spaces.

In Christianity, a similar term to dharma exists, physis. Physis was a primordial goddess, meaning, origin from the beginning, the crack, a cracked egg, or the embodiment of the cosmos through a limitation. When the cosmos (divine) wants to experience itself, it's done through an origin goddess. Physis means the first born. It is through your conception and birth that the cosmos are represented here on earth. The moment of your origin story, your conception, limitation supposedly began; however, what truly began was the experience of the divine through your being. The supposed limitation and castration at conception and in the body is linked to your divinity and your dharma. You're here to represent the divine in the present, alive and in the body. The moment you are castrated, the moment you are given a body, you have started your dharma.

Physics explains the ordinary world, and metaphysics, explains the extraordinary world. You can't separate them; they are within each other. In the Greek Bible or the Torah, *Nomos* is a word for law. The Bible says, don't live in accordance with divine law; divine law is all law. Spirit is not separate from matter. The body dies; it houses the spirit. Any extreme is against the law, because the law is trying to teach you to be in that temenos space.

Plato referred to *Eusebia*, the god of piety, not only to venerate God, not just a technical, spiritual godly practice or worship, but as linked to spiritual maturity. In my book *Spiritual Adulting*, every process becomes a reverential attitude toward life and the right conduct. If you have reverence in everything you do, whether it's parking the car, or pumping gas, you're going to live this Eusebia; you're going to live this dharma. You're going to live in right action and right thought. We need to learn to get there. This does come with age, yet it's not going to look the same at every moment. We have an earthly consciousness; we have a low-level animal nature, and we must accept that. Many people believe that living spiritually is only living in a high-consciousness state; however, we were given a low-level animal consciousness state for a reason. It is using both of these appropriately, that make us whole.

When I teach how to read the *Akashic Records,* one of the things I always say to people is, read the prayer with reverence. Every day, despite knowing it by heart, I read the prayer as it is intended, word for word, because it's reverence. There is a practice. Try to find some practice, if it's washing your car or blowing out your hair, and give it reverence. You have this idea of reverence in Eusebia in your life. The stoics have a term named *logos.* It means reason, rational and divine intelligence. It's the form and the spirit together, and that is the mind of God. Chronological time and divine or opportune time are always found together. We can't ever get out of the concept of time.

It depends on how we view time. That's why time appears to stretch, as Jung said, in a session. Because you're not bound to the clock when you're doing deep reverence work of your mind, of your body and of your spirit. You see this play of divine time, earthly time, spirit, and matter. Even in time, we can look at a lot of systems in terms of how ages are broken down.

For example, in Hinduism, there are four aims of life or goals of life: *dharma, artha, kama, moksha.* There is an *ashram* system of life. You buy into the system during your younger years. When you get older, you're going to go retire into the ashram, work on your soul, and achieve moksha or liberation. Dharma is always what you're doing, the task at hand. It's about being present and doing the duty at that moment. It's linked to piety, morality, and duties. It's not a spiritual practice, it's just a practice. The reverence is being mindful and present. Artha is when you accumulate wealth, health, and means. Wealth and health are always going to be together. Spirit and matter are always going to be together. Kama is linked to love, relationships, and emotions. You see, it's important to have relationships, whether sexual or otherwise. It's important to have some degree of wealth and health. Moksha means liberation, freedom and self-realization when you check yourself into the ashram to achieve moksha or liberation. Dharma and moksha do not have a specific age, phase, time, or place.

Deepak Chopra says, "Imagine that you are without physical form, a field of awareness everywhere always." We can't get out of our physical form. That would be dissociation, a mental disorder. What he's inviting us to do is to think that you're *beyond the form.* You're beyond the Saturn, you're beyond the limitations in your mind, and you're *everywhere, always.* It's a suggestion toward showing up as your divine being, even though you know that you're in a limited body. My theory, the *Triad of Dharma,* is shown below. Dharma is the form, the sustaining, the law, at the bottom of the triangle. *Rta* is truth, the refinement stages, at the base of the triangle next to dharma. At the tip of the triangle is *maya.* Maya is delusion or illusion. It's believing we are the form; it's believing we are our thoughts and believing we are what we have. One of the main functions of work is to realize that we are worthy just because, independent of a title, independent of a paycheck. This is a very sacred space if it gets us out of maya, out of illusion: if we don't get the promotion, if we do get the promotion, if our boss likes us, if our boss doesn't like us. We must use every person, place, thing, and situation as a mirror. The Law of Correspondence allows that we can be in a constant spiritual reverence and a constant spiritual adulting process, in our day-to-day life. You can live in the form, without delusion, but rather truth. Searching for your divine presence within the matter is the perfect opportunity to do spiritual work in a mundane setting.

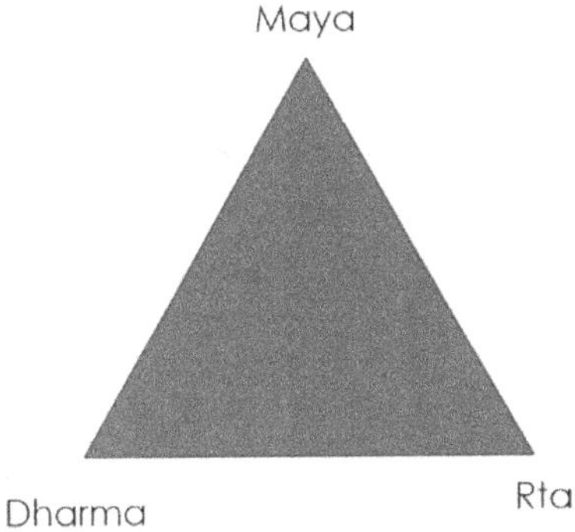

The Triad of Dharma: Dharma is the form, the sustaining, the law, at the bottom of the triangle. Rta is truth, the refinement stages, at the base of the triangle next to dharma. At the tip of the triangle is maya. Maya is delusion or illusion. It's believing we are the form; it's believing we are our thoughts and believing we are what we have.

Indriya is a concept from Ayurveda meaning faculties. It's linked to Indra, the goddess that holds back the chaos in the structure. Indriyas are faculties or senses and the way we experience the divine in the body. Indra is the chief deity of strength and power, therefore, it's through balance, only achieved from balancing spirit and matter, that you have the strength, the power, the divine will in its purest form. The definition of health in Ayurveda and the World Health Organization is linked to mind, body, spirit, and social well-being. We cannot eliminate the social aspect of health. A big component of your social interactions, of your rituals, happen at the coffee pot or at the lunch table. Trying to eliminate work from any of this is nonsense, because that's where you're spending most of your day. Indriya technically translates as your senses or faculties. Spiritual faculties, the faculties that control you, control your speech, your right mind, your right thought, your right action. We cannot separate form. We cannot understand the magnitude of the universe, of our own divine nature, without form. We need form in which to see it. If we judge the form, it's linked to ourselves judging our imperfect nature. Indriya is the principle of the spirit within, the appropriate use of the spiritual and material faculties.

There's something special about aging and wisdom, learning to use your senses for your benefit rather than to self-destruct. Desire is found in the body. If we honor our desires, through use of the senses, 100 percent of the time, we self-destruct. The idea of spirit and matter is to use the senses for pleasure (matter) 50 percent of the time, and the senses for spirit 50 percent of the time. The way to use the senses for spirit is the Greek concept of the Graces and Muses. This is how we experience God, or the spirit, in the earthly form, without self-destructing. In Greek mythology, the Muses allow us to experience God or the divine through the senses. You can experience god through your senses, rather than using your senses to self-destroy. This is the wisdom that comes with age, and that's where you get healthier as a result of the age, the senex, or the right use of mind, body, spirit, and social well-being. Alice Bailey in the *Labors of Hercules* says, "For far too long, the body, the physical, was the root of all evil, when it really is our narrow minds, hard small hearts, that causes wrong attitudes, and habits. The body is just the automatic response to the inner man."

Five Tenets for Being Zen

There was a Zen master in 1237 named Dōgen who wrote five tenets for being Zen: Take joy in service; treat each thing as the body of the Buddha; refuse judgments and preferences; do the best job that you can, and; become one with your activity. We can employ these in our work environment. In our day-to-day, we use them because everything's obviously sacred and spiritual, but specifically we can apply these in our day-to-day at work.

Take joy in service. Treat each thing as the body of the Buddha. You can substitute Buddha for whatever godhead or thing you believe in. Taking joy in service is identifying that you're both matter and spirit.

Refuse judgments and preferences. Don't judge that people with higher titles or better quality of life are better than you or they should be treated differently.

Do the best job that you can, and become one with your activity. See the service and generosity within the work that you're doing. Even though it's your job, go beyond time and space of the form, because it's serving your spirit, or at least that's the intention.

As you work, your offering may be small. Dōgen said the true bond between us and the Buddha is born of the smallest offering made with sincerity. When your thoughts are pure, when you're acting with sincerity, *then* you're of service. No matter what, even if it's just handing someone a cup of coffee, or a utensil. Treat each thing as if it's the body of the buddha. Treat each thing with reverence. Dōgen quotes a Chinese Chan master: *"Use the property and possessions of the community as carefully as if they were your own eyes."* Ordinarily we are thinking only about completing our task at work so we can rest or get praised for how good a job we've done. Let's try more sincere actions and more reverence. As we get beat down a bit from life, we start realizing it all matters. This is about learning how to treat such things that we allow the ineffable to manifest through them.

We have those things in our life that matter to us. It might be your purse; it might be your favorite pair of shoes. Imagine if you extrapolated that out to everything. Then we'd see a lot more sacredness in people, places, things, and situations. What helps me is knowing that every person, place, thing, or situation I create offers a lesson. There's something there for me to learn. Treat everything and everyone as quality. There are things that we consider junk. A Target t-shirt, oh, it's just a five-dollar t-shirt; but treat that as equal to your fifty-dollar Nordstrom t-shirt. Start trying to understand that everything is a representation and manifestation of the sacred; material and spiritual can't be separated. Your attitudes are going to change because everything is going to be important, and everyone's going to be important. It's not just going to be their quality or their title. It does not matter that someone signs your checks. It's important that we learn that version of humility.

You could be efficient and still be mindful; mindful does not mean slow. This is also an opportunity to not be controlling and a perfectionist. Perfection doesn't exist. If you can delegate some of your responsibilities, preferably at work but also at home, then you're learning detachment. The purpose of life is learning how to die. Learning to detach from things that no longer serve us, either forced or because we've exhausted the lesson is the domain of Saturn. As we own our inner authority, what I call our inner *s-ageist,* applying the wisdom earned, is the true gift of life.

Become one with the work. Look at the refinement process as your vocation as you get older.

CHAPTER 4
Dethroning Conformity

There's a big push these days for service leadership, with the employees at the top and the shareholders or stakeholders at the bottom. Robert Greenleaf, the original mastermind behind Servant Leadership, states that a "servant-leader is servant first" and holds certain tenants that are important, for instance: 1) leadership is an opportunity to serve others; 2) shares power and control; 3) measures success through growth and development and; 4) understands it's not about them. Traditional leadership has contrasting concepts such as: 1) seeing leadership as a rank to obtain; 2) power and control drive performance; 3) measures success through output and; 4) believes it's about them. I offer a "Self as Service" leadership model, and rather than a triangle I offer a wholistic perspective of leadership resembled by a wheel.

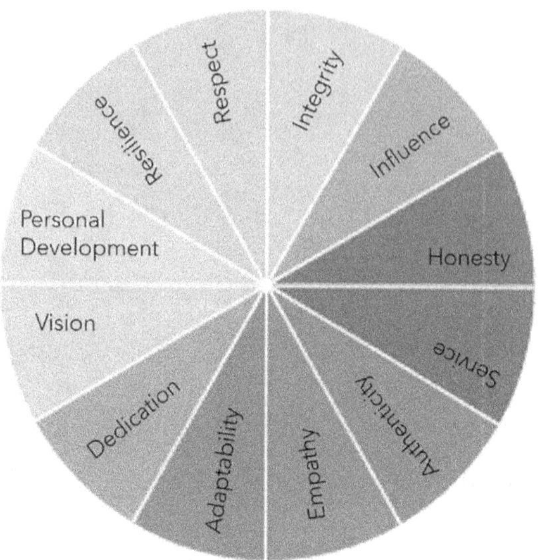

The "Self as Service" Leadership Wheel: A circle representing the twelve values of a leader, who gives and receives simultaneously. The aspects are linked to the astrological wheel. The sixth value is service, which is linked to the astrological house of Virgo, ruling work, day-to-day routine, health, illness, diet, purification and service.

The astrology wheel has twelve sections. The second house, the sixth house and the tenth house are called the earth houses. The earth element is anything to do with the earthly world. Time, money, and resources are the currency of self-worth in the earthly world. They're finite; there's not unlimited time, money, and resources. Your self-worth is linked to how you manage your time, your money, and your resources. A big part of why we work is to learn to value all three of these.

The sixth house is directly linked to stress and workplace illness. We have a body, thoughts, emotions, value systems, beliefs, and consciousness levels. Your employer is hiring all of you. We can't ignore that a big part of what causes problems in the workplace is stress, burnout, or increased and decreased productivity. We're smarter if we understand the person rather than just a job description or a paycheck. Work is a place for you to do spiritual work, not only gain material wealth. From the employee perspective or the employer perspective, we must see that we're hiring a whole person. The whole person shows up before they even get to the work.

Work serves us to become a better version of ourselves through the Law of Correspondence. Everything in your work environment is to teach you about your spiritual nature, to become a better, higher-consciousness-level human being. We can't break the individual up.

Most people do not know what their value system is. Your organization should have values; most of them have a mission and vision. Most places don't have real corporate values identified with the agency or company, which poses a problem. If you as an individual don't know your values, and the company doesn't have listed values, it's hard for you to identify if you have shared values. Most people hate their jobs, in part because they don't know what their values are. There's a major crisis if a company doesn't have a clear value system.

Virgo

Some consider Virgo, the ruler of the sixth house in astrology, which rules our work life, day-to-day operations and health, the most boring sign, because it's the commoner or everyman archetype. That's the meaning of the sixth house in astrology. The day-to-day—that's where everything happens.

The glyph of Virgo, referring to materia prima, or prima materia, an alchemical and philosophical concept that means first matter. First matter is the starting material, the body, required for humans to become the magnum opus, their divinity through form, as a result of their lived experiences. Virgo represents the land that needs to be tended to daily, the heaviness of the day-to-day and work life, where we learn to become the gold, our truest nature and divine essence.

Virgo is such an important space in our life, our work life. It seems day-to-day and boring, but has so much information symbolically. In the story of the Virgin Mary, she remains a virgin. Virgo represents the virgin. It's linked to the sixth house in astrology. The symbol for Virgo looks like the letters MP, which stands for *materia prima*, or first matter, referring to the primitive base required for all matter. We have some agency, in our day-to-day boring Virgo activities, to reap what we're going to sow, but it has to do with consistency. It has to do with stability and daily activities. Nobody likes boring.

Virgin Mary spiritually represents the womb for your spiritual consciousness growth. Work is sacred because the work is the day-to-day that you're tending to. The story of the Virgin Mary has a symbolic reference to do with our work life, once tended to with self-love can become the love as service to another. The symbolism of the mother's love, without any need for anything in return because we have met our own needs and love ourselves unconditionally. It has to do with what we're doing with the land that's raw, the *materia prima*, for us to build what we want on it. Virgin Mary, the sixth house, the day-to-day, houses our spiritual consciousness or Christ consciousness. Virgo is also called "the goddess of the two ways" because of the holy mother principle. She symbolizes matter, our body, work, money, but also the Christ aspect as our divine self. At work, you tend to and grow the seed of your Christ consciousness.

When we neglect our spiritual nature, we get sick. In astrology, the sixth house rules work and health as well as illness. When we're not using the work environment as a spiritual lesson or a sacred space, we open ourselves up to illness. There's something about the consistency of the day-to-day. Mindfulness means acting mindfully with our time, energy, and money. Spica is the brightest star in the Virgo constellation, and it means *ear of corn or bread*. Work gives us our daily bread. It's the place we go daily, and it's what gives us our money to eat our daily bread. It's also the place, if we use it correctly, where we can get our spiritual bread. Our spiritual nourishment, not just our financial nourishment. That's the intention, to really use work as a sacred space. Jesus is born in Bethlehem, which means *house of bread*. Virgo, the Virgin Mary, the workhouse, the day-to-day. Taking raw material, materia prima, and building something.

The rise of gluten intolerance, like illness in general, is to remind us that we are limited and human, and we need to create illness to keep us connected to the body. Because as we are narcissists (part divine), our tendency is to not want to be human and flawed. So gluten, being a wheat allergy, and wheat being the common grain and cheap back in the day, is an illness that psychologically is an attempt to be "above" the norm, not an everyday man, and only embody the Jesus archetype of the divine, and negate the human aspect.

If you don't bend, you break. Conformity involves a request—someone requesting you do something, going along with people of equal status, and relies on the need to be socially accepted. Obedience is something you're told to do, involves an order, and is usually from somebody of a higher rank. It relies on social power. Compliance is changing your behavior at the request of another person. One of the key experiments about conformity inquired, "To what extent will you go against your own convictions to fit in with the crowd?" Studies show we conform to social pressure, yet we think that we don't. One of the most famous psychological experiments on obedience was the Milgram experience. Actors were hired to pretend to be study subjects getting shocked for wrong answers. The real study subjects were those administering the shocks as authority figures insisted the they shock the actors despite dangerously high voltage. The Milgram experiment showed how surprisingly obedient people are to authority.

Many historical events, like those heading the concentration camps have accepted authority blindly. Accepting limitations is part of the lesson of Saturn and life, but you need to have your own value system. Learn to cultivate that inner s-ageist, the inner authority rather than looking for it externally. Philip Zimbardo, a professor at Stanford University, conducted another famous psychological experiment on role paly and authority. Zimbardo recruited Stanford University students to either play a role as a prison guard or as a prisoner. The prison guards had taken their roles so seriously, they genuinely started believing they were prison guards and their fellow classmates were inmates! After six days the study was shut down due to mistreatment towards the pretend inmates.

We often mistake our roles for who we are and forget our true nature. Allison, a long-time client, shared a dream about a man bringing her entangled cables and headsets. The headsets and cables resembled the roles she was identifying with and were getting in her way to finding her true vocation. We must organize our roles and find our truc selves. Pull away your role as mother, wife, daughter, teacher and political activist. Roles are what you do, not who you are.

Many people readily accept the influence of an authority, even when it means causing potential harm to another person. Charles Hofling in 1966 created a version of the Milgram experience with hospital nurses. Without knowing, the nurse on duty was asked to administer 20mg of a fake medication called *Astroten* to a patient named Mr. Jones when the nurse knew the maximum dosage was 10 mg. The order was given over the phone and no paperwork had been administered and drugs are not allowed to exceed their maximum dosage, all violations of the hospital; yet, over 95% of the experimental study nurses were ready to administer the medication based on the authority of the physician. It's scary to go against the grain. There are two types of obedience: situational obedience versus dispositional obedience. What situation do you find yourself in that's situational obedience? There are times that you must obey, based on a situation. We've all been there. You're not going to yell at the cop. You're going to just say, *"Yes sir, I'm sorry sir, give me the ticket sir."*

Another situation in which you deal with others is dispositional obedience. This is where your values come in; this is linked to what type of person you are. Dispositional obedience is going to show up as integrity and how you show up in your day-to-day. Removal of responsibility encourages obedience. I must live by my mantra, "Take personal responsibility." I take responsibility for my failures, as much responsibility as I take for my successes—and we don't want to do that.

We don't want to take responsibility for our failures or our successes. We're constantly looking for some magic, someone to give the credit to. We're not allowed to take credit for our successes, and we surely don't want to take credit for our failures. That's what leads to obedience. We were told to be humble, not prideful. By cultivating your inner authority, you'll know when to do either, appropriately. People are playing small, rather than owning up to their pride and their ambition. That's what I call transcendental narcissism. We hide, pretending we don't want recognition and that we are about service and social justice, which leads to burnout. However, the tribal narcissists, they want the recognition, own their pride, but then don't own their shadow or failures. Neither of these are balanced. We must take credit for success and failure. For health we need to identify our shadow and take credit for our successes, not pretend we have no pride or ambition. Personal responsibility boils down to your value system. If you don't have clear values, a rulebook, or philosophy of life, ultimately, it's all the same, you cannot move in the world as an adult. Surely you can't become a spiritual adult.

We need to get really clear on our rulebook, on our philosophy of life, on our values. This brings me to the organization that you work for. What is their value statement? What is their mission statement? What is their vision statement? A mission statement and vision statement are very existential. It's very larger than life; it's like your vocation. What do you want to do in the world? Someone told me, "I want to bring light to the world." That's a vision statement. Your vision of what you want to do. What is the goal of your life from an earthly perspective? Are you working in a company that supports your goals, your missions, your values? If not, of course you're going to be sick. Edward de Bono said, "Effectiveness without values is a tool without a purpose." In your job or in your life, what are you being effective in? What's the value? We're trying to live our spiritual lives and our material lives without having these sorts of conversations. Without values, it is a tool that has no purpose. Imagine if I have a tool and I don't even know what it's for. That's how most of us are living our life. You are a tool for humanity, for your family, for your partners, for your friends, yet you don't know how to use yourself. It's sad, but this is what you're going to find.

Company culture is formed based on core principles; it should guide the employee and the company. What are your goals? How do they align with the company's goals? They often say, what can you bring to the table? It should go back to values and the question should be: how is the company going to serve me? It should be a mutual relationship, but we don't have these conversations. Part of what happens in your job and why there's so much job dissatisfaction is that it's not in alignment with your values. You must check the values of yourself, which you must know, and the alignment of the organization with your values. If I work at this organization and there's something severely in violation with my rules, with my values, my philosophy of life, I cannot work here. That is self-betrayal; that is death. It is time to exit at that point. Have your exit strategy. Work sociology is defined as the goal of being productive in a way that meets human needs. That's the spiritual aspect of your work: how does it meet your needs, and how does it meet the needs of others? A vocation is considered a calling. Its origins were in religious life, but now it is a calling or a divine purpose, linked to the higher virtues. The vocation; that's the higher virtue.

Byron Katie, a modern-day spiritual teacher and Ivan G. Gurdjieff, an Armenian philosopher, both developed spiritual systems called "the Work". There is a reason spirituality is "work," just like earthly work. It may not give you money in the end, but it'll give you wealth. It will definitively give you virtue, satisfaction, and vocation, but there may not be a wealth payoff in the monetary sense. Your earthly work is using sacred space, setting boundaries, being clear, realizing that the team supports you and helps you will lead to this spiritual work. These are what I call process wins, rather than outcome wins, and they're spiritual in nature because they build your astral body and raise your consciousness.

Gurdjieff's main premise was as in many spiritual philosophies, that man is asleep to his true nature. We are unaware of our divine nature, and instead we associate ourselves with our role identity. What we need is unified consciousness. There is a place for earthly consciousness, our job titles and monetary gains; however, remembering our divine state is equally as important. A key tenet in his work is his theory of "multiple I's". He considered the human being to have multiple I's within himself which causes conflict within. I call this an incongruence. There are many fragmented parts within us, and we attempt to live healthy lives despite these fragments. The subconscious often splits these fragments off and we pretend they don't exist, rather they become shadow aspects of ourself and cause damage. The goal of unified consciousness is to integrate the fragmented parts and unify them so we are whole beings, despite the incongruencies in our psyche. At work, through the various projections of the shadow, our work family mirrors the archetypes of fragmented parts and as we identify they are simply unintegrated aspects of ourselves we can begin to become whole and remember our true earthly and divine nature.

Byron Katie says to ask yourself four questions. Think of a thought that you have that's negative about yourself. The first question is, "*Is it true?*" What's a thought you're having about yourself? Is it negative? "*I have a bad temper, is it true?*" The second question is, "*Can you absolutely know that it's true?*" No! You never can never know that something is a hundred percent true. Jessica, a client, stated that everyone gossips about her. But nobody has ever in their life uttered a bad word about you. They're just a simple reflection of self, a mirror. Your thoughts are misleading. Your thoughts serve for information, and they lead you to judgments. Your thoughts lead you to values, but you can't believe every single thought that you have because it's not true. The third question in Byron Katie's model is, "How do you react when you believe that thought about yourself?" This is linked to an emotion. Each impure thought is attached to negative emotion learned in the womb. We want to prove a negative thought right so we can subconsciously return to the womb; thereby we attach a negative emotion to the thought and 'poof', we are there! The fourth question is, "Who would you be without that thought?" You'd be heading towards spiritual adulting and spiritual adulting implies you're not a child of anyone. You can meet your own needs and love yourself unconditionally, this is a scary and lonely thought. Work implies the earthly work of a paycheck, but also the inner work of the spirit and the soul. We must cultivate our consciousness, we must cultivate the *materia prima,* the land (holy grail) where our soul dwells. To cultivate the holy grail which is our body, we must begin to process thoughts properly to avoid illness and burnout.

Dethroning Greed

In the 1987 movie "Wall Street," Michael Douglas as Gordon Gekko gave a speech where he said, "Greed, for lack of a better word, is good." The definition of greed is "a selfish and excessive desire for more of something, such as money." Most greed definitions speak in terms of food or money; however, we never look at greed in terms of thoughts. Our thoughts are greedy; we hoard thoughts and the emotions and desires that accompany them. Removal of a desire is not enough, if we do not look at the thought behind our desires, we are greedy by holding on to the thoughts and can never achieve detachment. Thoughts are material in nature. Just because you cannot "see" them, they have weight and cause pressure. Similar to the way we measure air with barometric pressure, we can measure thoughts with how they materialize in our life as conflict or in the body as illness.

German social psychologist, Erich Fromm says greed is "a bottomless pit which exhausts the person in an endless effort to satisfy the need without ever reaching satisfaction."

If you were hungry, you might kill someone for a piece of bread, and your hunger may be satiated for a few hours. However, our thoughts and their associated emotions are relentless and the subconscious desire behind them is to be loved unconditionally. Since this can never be satisfied by another we create conflict or illness in an attempt to reach a point of satisfaction. It will never happen. Unconditional love is an inside job; therefore, attempting to get your needs met by another is greed and will never lead to satisfaction. We are in a vicious cycle of what I call psychological homeostasis. Your negative thoughts and emotions drive you to fulfill a need through another person or an external validation, this is the homeostasis of the mind; however, physical homeostasis aims to keep your body stable and helps you, psychological homeostasis is harmful because you're outsourcing love and needs that cannot be satisfied externally. The antidote to the greediness of your thoughts, and subsequent emotions, is to have a very clear value system.

Identifying a clear value system for each pillar of life, is the answer to slowing the subconscious greed for more and more; however, failing to define your values in definable, measurable and observable terms is greedy.

Most people don't know their top values, therefore, attempting to define them in observable, measurable terms is a struggle, but proves to be one of the most powerful techniques in achieving self-worth and contentment. The question I pose is: what are your top two values, and it cannot be family? When the conversation starts it's easy to spit out answers like loyalty, integrity and community, for example; however, when the specifics of defining the terms in observable and measurable terms is posed, the lack of honesty in which we live our life and our self-betrayal, becomes evident. This inability to define your value system is greed. We hold on to the limiting thoughts from childhood as a subconscious attempt to belong to our families, once we define our values we can detach from faulty thinking and live as spiritual adults. However, to the psyche, this disruption of the psychological homeostasis feels like death. At the moment of conception you inherit one impure thought that reinforces your unworthiness. If you attempt to raise consciousness around that thought, eliminate the unworthiness, it's as if you cease to exist. The greed sets in because in every situation that causes conflict, no matter how small, the thread of worthlessness is present. You will prove this thought true over and again to gain love and belonging needs (symbolically) and as a reminder that you were conceived, created, wanted and alive. It's truly dysfunctional to use a limiting thought as a link to living; however, the subconscious knows no other way. The 0-100 thinking is greedy and is related to proving that the limiting thought exists 100% of the time.

One way the soul attempts to redirect our greed is through illness. Illness is a direct result of greed. When we fail to process painful thoughts, emotions and desires they accumulate in the energy field, eventually taking over the physical body.

It's an attempt to stop living in denial and face our self-betrayal head on. If our time, energy and resources are simply spent in seeking external validation, being useful to other's so we are somewhat loved, the soul redirects the priorities through illness. Illness is a manifestation of something deeper in the subconscious that isn't sitting well with you. Illness is often the soul's last attempt to get your attention. In Shamanism, the sick person is often initiated into shamanism through their illness. The accumulation of years of self-betrayal and violating your boundaries energetically accumulate and show up in the body as illness. Illness is the psyche's last attempt to get you to listen. In Christian Fleche's model called Biodecoding® he believes the symptoms we experience in the body are linked to mental and emotional programming that need to be addressed. For example, I had breast cancer for six years. During my divorce and custody battle I buried the pain in an attempt to continue working and living an apparently normal life; however, the psychological and emotional pain was never addressed. According to Biodecoding® my left breast indicated unresolved issues linked to motherhood, I understood I needed to go deep into the subconscious programming that was linked to my unworthiness as a mother.

If we don't process our thoughts, emotions, and desires, we never let go. We remain attached to childhood programming as an attempt to belong to the family or tribe. When you set limits on someone and offer clear directives and establish boundaries, you make that person feel safe. You make yourself safe. There are four unmet needs from childhood we all have: safety and security; protection; validation, and; love and belonging. The most important one is safety. Our parents failed to provide safe environments because they lacked clarity and precise rule books. We all suffered incongruencies which makes our psyche's a dangerous place. If we actually stop to think about what we are thinking, we would identify the lack of safety from childhood which confirms we are unlovable and don't have permission to feel safe within ourselves. Impure thoughts don't go away; however, learning to process them can avoid most illnesses and offer insight to our values and how to create safe spaces within ourselves. Attachment is the root of all suffering said the Buddha. He was referring to thoughts and the emotions attached to those thoughts. We refuse to set boundaries and a clear value system because if we let our limiting thoughts and emotions go, who will we belong to? We are attached symbolically and energetically to our family of origin, no matter how far you run or how dysfunctional it was; therefore, it is how our love and belonging needs are met. The subconscious wants you to self-betray by not establishing boundaries or a clear value system thereby getting your love and belonging needs met, albeit dysfunctionally.

Unprocessed thoughts and emotions are extra baggage, and overtime cause illness, stress and burnout. By setting clear boundaries and transparency in conversations, we show up for ourselves and meet our own needs and give the other person the right to do the same. This is the safety need we all lacked in childhood, and makes it uncomfortable to live in this way; however, safety is the need most associated with love. Ironically, because our childhood homes were not safe, with clarity and transparency, we shun this version of love and find it harsh. Not setting limits, not having a clear value system, not having any sort of directives or clear measurable qualities around a value really is just another form of greed or attachment. Staying in the story feeds the mental and emotional hunger we all have, but doesn't lead to mental or physical health.

One of my favorite sayings is, "an adult asks for what they want and the other adult has a right to say no." However, we aren't clear in our requests for fear of losing a version of love that is never satisfactory. To identify the love we get from attachment to our negative thoughts and emotions, I created a personal TED talk clients can use as inner dialogue when conflict arises. The best way to work through impure thoughts and conflicts is to talk yourself though a personal TED talk. TED is not associated with the famous Ted Talk program, it is simply an acronym for thoughts, emotions and desires, and when done properly can immediately diffuse conflict. The personal TED talk, is just three easy questions you ask yourself when any stress arises. It shows you how you created the conflict and the story or belief you are choosing to hold on to to remain "loved" by your tribe or family of origin. No matter how silly it sounds, we don't detach from these negative thoughts or emotions, because we feel comforted by them and that we at least belong somewhere, and to something.

The personal TED talk consists of asking yourself three questions when a conflict arises:

1. Does the thought most resemble your mother or father?
2. What don't I like about the conflict?
3. What does it prove about me when I create this conflict? Name the emotion.

Once you identify the TED talk that you're holding on to is a thought and an emotion that was inherited by your parents, you begin to realize that you hold on to these self-destructive tendencies simply to feel love and belonging. When you identify what you don't like about the conflict, you can begin to see that you're judging yourself, not the other and by judging yourself, again you're holding on to a story and a false narrative from your family of origin. Simply processing the conflict with a personal TED talk diffuses the energy pressure and build up and allows room for change. Jung said "there is no coming to consciousness without pain.", The pain is identifying that we are creating our conflicts and our reality from a place of unprocessed thoughts, emotions and desires. Pain is necessary, we all have pain, suffering is optional. That's the victim; that's the innocent archetype. Jung also said, "People will do anything no matter how absurd to avoid facing their own soul, one does not become enlightened by imagining figures of light, but by making the darkness conscious." It's in the darkness that we're going to truly bring that to the light. Thomas Aquinas said, "we must will the truth, stand in light, and seek our own truth and not something false." It is difficult to imagine taking responsibility for every thought; however, if not, that energy will be materialized as conflict inside or outside the body.

An illness might provide us a reason to search further for our true self. We seek illness to get closer to the truth, to accept our body more so that the divine can work through us in a balanced state. It's through illness that we may learn to limit our earthly power so our divine can come through. Is it greedy to get sick? Is it greedy to use resources? Is it greedy to have time off, so to speak, so that we can do this work? I want to know, will we do anything to face our soul with permission, even become ill? Jung says people will do anything, no matter how absurd, to avoid facing their own soul. Maybe if we haven't been given permission societally, we don't have that option. Maybe we're actually so programmed, like Thomas Aquinas says, to seek our soul and find our truth that we need permission, and the only sort of societal permission is illness.

For example, 1.6 million workers suffered work-related ill health between 2019 and 2020. More than half of those workers suffered from stress, depression, and anxiety. Anxiety is linked to validation needs. Unprocessed thoughts materialize in the body and creates anxiety.

Thirty percent of work-related illnesses are musculoskeletal disorders. Musculoskeletal disorders are related to the structure of one's life. Often what the psyche is screaming is "my life needs to collapse" so I can rebuild on a new foundation". Oftentimes, these disorders linked to the structure of one's life involve needing clarity, boundaries, and a clear value system. We often need permission to process our impure thoughts, emotions, and desires; the break we get from a breakdown allows the realization that the current life's structure is inauthentic and false.

The Sick Role and Illness Behavior

The Sick Role concept was developed by American researcher and sociologist Talcott Parsons in 1951. He saw the sick role as a form of deviance, or going against societal expectations because ill people have different patterns of behavior than the norm. You have exemption from normal responsibilities, and because you're sick, you're not blamed for the illness. This is linked even to people with lifestyle diseases based on their obesity or sedentary lifestyle. Parsons discusses the idea of a sick role, a term which he describes as the social aspects and the privileges of falling ill. We don't think of it in this way, that it's a privilege, with an obligation which accompanies it. Parson goes on to say that a sick individual takes on the role of the sanctioned deviant, meaning that the sufferer is not a functional member of society during the time of their illness. Deviants must be policed, which is the role of a doctor or medical professional.

In 1962, Dr. David Mechanic defines *illness behavior* in his landmark paper, "The Concept of Illness Behavior," in the *Journal of Chronic Diseases*, as the ways in which given symptoms may be differentially perceived, evaluated and acted (or not acted) by different persons. There are a range of behaviors that are highly individualistic and variable. This is directly linked to how your parents took care of you when you were sick, what you were allowed to do, how the hierarchy shifted, and how you were "off the hook" when you were sick.

The process of perceiving and assigning meaning to symptoms is a growing business. Biodecoding, bioneuroemotion, shamanism are just some fields that have emerged (or existed) linking spiritual and energetic and emotional meanings to illness. As rabbi and philosopher Moses Maimonides stated "accept the truth from whatever source it comes." The symptoms mean something: they're teaching me a lesson. I help clients bio-decode the message based on the side of the body, the organ and the function. In addition to the anatomical symbology, there are other things intertwined with values and beliefs. Pain itself may become the focus of the self and the self-identity, and it may be viewed as tangential to the person. Pain is a role, and it plays a role in defining your identity. There is attachment to the illness in every introduction:

"I'm diabetic," "I have a gluten allergy," or "I have depression." We see this identification with that illness as a role that someone wears almost like a proud vest. In Christian tradition and in other spiritual traditions, pain and suffering is a belief system and often revered. In astrology, the sixth house, which again rules work, health, and illness, also rules purification. It is through the body that we purify any unprocessed thoughts, emotions and desires.

Labors and Truths

In Greek mythology, Hercules was the illegitimate son of Zeus and hated by Hera. As a result, Hera forced him to complete twelve labors before he could return home to Olympus and sit by his father's side. Hercules' journey, represents our own hero's journey. The twelve tasks represent the labors we must fulfill as a spiritual aspirant to return home to the universal consciousness. They happen only on earth, in an embodiment and they reunite our physical nature with our spiritual nature. In my book *Spiritual Adulting*, I use the twelve labors as the foundation of my spiritual adulting program. Each labor correlates with a truth we must seek and accept to become whole, unified beings.

Truth Six, is the Truth of Purification and correlates to Hercules retrieving the Girdle of Hippolyte. Hippolyte was the Queen of the Amazons and wore a chastity girdle. When Hercules went to retrieve it, he accidentally killed her, because he failed to listen to Hippolyte. In shock, he went and purified his actions by saving Hesione who was drowning nearby. This labor represents our inability to listen to our true impure thoughts, mistreating our bodies as a result and purifying our poor choices with abstinence or a cleanse. This vicious cycle is how we live addicted to our suffering and our minds and bodies are at odds. Our impure thoughts are purified through our bodies. Learning to process thoughts will lessen the damage to our bodies and overtime keep us healthier. The currency of self-worth is linked to how we spend our energy. There are five measures of self-worth in the earthly consciousness and misuse of any speaks to our self-betrayal and honoring our thoughts of unworthiness. The subconscious is calculating each time you self-betray and you "pay up", what I call a sacrifice, in one of five areas within 24-48 hours after an offense. Every impure thought that is not processed through a TED talk will affect our lives in overdoing one of five areas: sex, money, time, food (drugs/alcohol) and health/illness. If you begin to track your thoughts of self-betrayal, you will begin to see your pattern emerge. DO you overpay? Do you violate your time commitments? Track an of these five areas back to the impure thought and how you self-betrayed and violated your value system and you'll have a clear map of how like Hercules you make an offense and attempt to purify it. Continuous misuse of the body to process thoughts and using purification is self-destructive and will eventually make you sick. The cycle is a vicious 0-100 cycle and is greedy. Once we identify the pattern, we can stop hurting ourselves with the 0 to 100 pendulum swings of cleansing and purifying behaviors after a bender, and rather, slow the swings, process the thoughts with the TED talk, and accept we are human and we don't need perfection and purification, we need acceptance.

General Adaptation Syndrome

Hans Selye created a three-stage model called GAS, general adaptation syndrome, to explain stress. First there's an alarm that shocks you, then you hold that level of resistance, and your body gets exhausted. We're in a constant fight or flight, or stress cycle, because of our emotional greed. Our subconscious is that greedy child seeking a way to get its needs met constantly. This is the true stress that is occurring behind the guise of deadlines and traffic jams. Using this model and this concept of GAS, I explain to clients that the purification or the illness is gas (or a fart) in the psychological system. We cannot sustain this level of psychological stress and perfection. Our inner child must fart, which leads us to overindulgence in one of 5 areas (food or alcohol, sex, money, time or illness), and then we cycle back again to purify ourselves for the fart or overindulgence and again attempt perfection. When you have a stress problem, it builds; oftentimes it's one hundred on the zero-to-one-hundred pendulum swings of the psyche. When we show up as the one hundred in our script, it's often linked to perfection in the earthly realm: exercise, diet, work. The release in the system, the gas, comes as a detriment in the areas of food (or other addictions or poor coping skills like alcohol), money, time, sex and illness.

In my Hidden Truths ™ program, I teach clients that illnesses are materialized thoughts and emotions that have not been fully processed. When impure thoughts and emotions aren't accepted they form energetic bricks that the body holds onto. Eventually, overtime, those energetic bricks become illness. Illnesses are either feminine or masculine, depending on the location on the body. The feminine lineage is represented on the left and the masculine lineage on the right. Feminine illness may represent the mother and children, while masculine illnesses represent the romantic aspects of life. Illnesses are also scarcity or abundant in nature. Illnesses that grow, like tumors, indicate the person wants more of something, while scarcity illnesses like osteoporosis, the person desires less of something. My breast cancer was on the left side and I deduced I wanted more time with my children after my custody battle. Another question to ask is "*What is the function of the organ?*" The function of the organ is linked to the impure thought the person is working through. I was questioning my motherhood and my breast was affected. Clients with structural issues are often questioning the entire structure of their lives and the vertebrae are affected. The organs are vibrationally attuned to the impure thoughts and the physical organs hold space for the thoughts until they become fully processed. Illness may be the only socially acceptable way to process impure thoughts and the meaning of life; therefore, it plays an important role in society.

Desiree, a client, has Parkinson's disease, a disorder of the central nervous system that affects movement and includes tremors. Issues related to the are thoughts that are unable to materialize in the body because there is an underlying belief that the roots are unsafe. Roots often refer to the family structure. Embodying fully is considered unsafe; therefore, the nervous system creates movement (Parkinson's, anxiety etc.…) to subconsciously not lay roots and be in constant movement and fight or flight as a psychological attempt to keep "safe" from laying down roots. The core issue is not wanting to take full responsibility for low-level consciousness. Desiree is tired of carrying all the weight of the family. She received validation from organizing the chaos and being the go-to problem solver, the mover and shaker of solving family problems. As we work together to process the thoughts and emotions linked to her validation needs and her self-worth, her symptoms improve after each session.

Thoughts are materialized in the body. If you never let go of your thoughts, emotions and desires, you get sick, and it's greedy; therefore, illness serves as a way to break the dysfunction of the system and let go of unprocessed thoughts and emotions in a socially acceptable way. Can you envision a world where we simply hold space for another who is having a few bad months, who needs to not be socially accommodating so he can tend to his wounds? If we are capable of creating this world, we can minimize the need for at least one function that illness serves.

Narcissists

Another function of illness is to help what I call transcendental narcissists re-enter the body. There are two types of narcissists, transcendental and tribal. This is not Narcissitic Personality Disorder (NPD), a mental illness in the DSM-5 defined as a pervasive pattern of grandiosity, need for admiration and a lack of empathy. This term is in reference to Narcissus, the hunter known for his beauty in Greek mythology. The character in this myth is the origin of the term narcissism, a fixation with oneself. Since we cannot serve others until the third stage of Kohlberg's theory, in essence, we are all narcissists. In the twelve labors of Hercules, it is not until the eleventh labor that Hercules begins thinking about another and starts to serve humanity. Likewise, most of our actions are self-serving in an attempt to lead to the individuation process. Transcendental narcissists live in the higher chakras. There tends to be a trauma, perhaps early on, that caused them to disassociate from the body because it is too painful. These clients tend to come to my practice seeking transcendental experiences and with a true desire to reach enlightenment; however, enlightenment can only happen in the body, so we focus on embodiment practices. The reason I call them transcendental narcissists is because if we are only seeking transcendence, we are subconsciously trying to avoid the fact that we are human. Usually linked to an early traumatic experience, the body is a source of pain, so healing only comes through embodiment. Embodiment requires a realization of impure thoughts, often linked to sins, passions or vices, which is judged as the antithesis of enlightenment, but rather, is the only path through. It is through the darkness one can appreciate the light. Transcendental narcissists also tend to enjoy pain as pleasure. They value or even idealize suffering and tend to embody a Jesus or savior-martyr-rescuer archetype. One of the few ways to help embody a transcendental narcissist is via illness.

Tribal narcissists are those that tend to seek pleasure as pain, perhaps overdoing the pleasures and desires of the flesh and probably motivated by the lower chakras and earthly pleasures; the spiritual aspect of their lives is an afterthought. Illness serves to create a space and identify perhaps that sex, money, indulgence isn't all that life has to offer, so illness creates that space to work on their spiritual lives. The midpoint between the transcendental and tribal narcissist is the third chakra, the center of self and self-worth. Chiron, the Greek mythology centaur, represents the human and the animal consciousness that we all have as humans. Living in either all lower consciousness, or tribal narcissism, just like living in all divine consciousness (or trying to) or transcendental narcissism, leads to illness, the most common need for purification in the psyche. Technically it's all in the psyche. We think purifying the body will clean the impure thoughts, but it doesn't. If we don't enter the subconscious, the shadow and the impure thoughts we are judging, the body purification is useless.

Power Currencies

In my book, *The Truth is in the Triangle: The Hidden Truths on how to Achive Wholeness in Relationships* I explain there are two power currencies: overt and covert. You learned your preferred power currency during your young years between zero and seven. The first moment of shame that you can remember is linked to the parent with the power currency you later adopt as an adult. The impure thought and emotion attached to the moment of shame; thereby creating your power currency, is difficult to reconcile in the psyche. How could I want to benefit from the exact power currency that shamed me and caused my childhood trauma? For example, when I was six I threw garbage in the neighbor's pool and I was severely punished for it. I identified an overt power currency in my parents, yelling and screaming, and my subconscious identified that as the power that would get me ahead. In another example, Jones, a client of mine who is homosexual, came out at a very young age. There was no yelling and screaming; rather, his parents ignored what he said, and he identified a covert, manipulative power currency as the way to gain power in the world. Everyone has both, but we have a preferred power currency. At work we tend to judge those with the opposite style, instead it's a mirror of what we need to integrate. Therefore, the purification process occurs by enduring others in the workspace with the opposite power currency. Saturn's mission is to cause you to bend and be flexible and realize you need both, depending on the situation; hence, discernment.

The workspace is where you'll encounter your opposite power currency that will teach you discernment and balance. If you're covert, then you might not like the overt personalities. If you're overt, you might really dislike the covert personalities. You're there to try and learn the other currency so that you can be in balance, bend and conform as needed, depending on the situation. Become the one that you need to be. There's not one way to do it all the time. That's discernment. Some believe that being spiritual or the better person is being covert; however, if you cannot process the thoughts and emotions associated with it then you're ignoring the issue in the name of avoidance. This is not more spiritual. There are times where overt power is absolutely appropriate and the most spiritual thing to do. Even Jesus in John 2:16 yelled "get these things out of here and stop turning my Father's house into a marketplace." I often tell clients they must bring the appropriate tool to the fight. You cannot bring a butter knife to a sword fight, you'll get slaughtered. There are times where overt power is necessary. Discerning which power currency to use, with who and when is one of the most spiritual concepts and contributes to self worth.

The Virgo archetype is learning to live as the divine, yet also be in the body with discernment and limitation. Virgo is the commoner or everyman archetype, work reminds us we all need to take care of body with food, exercise, sleep and work every day. It's the only house, sign and archetype that helps balance the narcissism and levels the playing field of every human, no matter their situation. It's the materia prima, there's nothing really exciting about the common or routine. It's day-to-day, it's boring. *I must eat every day, I must work every day, and there's no excitement.* You need that day-to-day routine, that discernment that work as a sacred space provides you.

As noted in my book Spiritual Adulting, around age 33 it is common to develop an illness or a problem that keeps you infirmed. 33 is linked to the commoner archetype, namely Jesus, and one the psyche's attempts to begin soul work. It sets a foundation for deeper spiritual work later on in life. Burnout has a lot to do with trying to live in the higher chakras, in the high consciousness; *I serve humanity,* the transcendental narcissist. Burnout has a lot to do with being checked out of the body. We're so burnt out because we're not in the body. We're living only in those higher chakras, we don't want to process thought and emotion.

Emotion needs to be processed through the body to feel a feeling. Emotion turns to feeling and you feel it. When clients tell me, "Frances, I was in bed for twelve hours after our session," or "I vomited," I'm like, that's great, you just felt your feeling. You took it from emotion, which is unprocessed greed, and you let go of it to materialize through the body. That's part of the function of the body: purification. Not in an abstinence or cleansing way, but rather by processing the impure thought fully. You've let it go; you've now felt the feeling. Feeling our feelings completely, instead of holding on to them for fear of the pain, can prevent larger illnesses like cancer and Parkinson's. Emotions are materialized thought, and eventually can cause tumors or degredation of the body, if not fully felt overtime. Burnout is directly linked to not doing that process, not using the body for real purification to feel the feelings, because you're only living in the higher chakras.

Dexter's entire musculoskeletal system broke down. She had injuries: her wrist and her neck broke. Everything structurally is absolutely a mess. She leans towards covert power and is a behind-the-scenes personality. She works on music sets and hands the big artists the guitars and water bottles. She wears black and prefers to hide out. Her illness screams, *notice me*. People scream very loud with the illnesses that they create. It's a form of manipulation, of covert power currency, to yell and scream silently. Structural illnesses are silent illnesses.

Some illnesses are scarcity illnesses and break down, versus others that build up in the body. The entire structure of the person collapses, in Dexter's case being the structure or the backstage orchestrator no longer works for her. Illness gives them permission to be the star of the show. These are illnesses that scream; they're hidden types of illnesses.

Other illness are more overt or abundant in nature. Cancer is growth and takes up space. They're both narcissistic, but in the psychology of the illness, one is more overt and the other more covert. You're doing more, or you're breaking down and screaming louder in a covert way. What disease do we all have? We all have the disease of feeling either omnipotent or not important. We are creating illness and dislike work because it's the body and the mundane day-to-day that makes us the common mortal we struggle with in the depths of the psyche. Brad Steiger wrote *Gods of Aquarius,* where he describes humans as part reptiles and special aliens. This is nonsense! In the current Age of Aquarius we hear of new categories of people: earth angels, star seeds, aliens, any attempt to not be boring and human.

Workaholics are greedy. You want more and you want more validation. If you're criticizing the laziness in another person, it's because you have it in yourself. If you're at work all the time and all you do is think about work, you clock out and you stay two more hours, or you neglect your family and your responsibilities at home, then you're lazy, too. You're just trying to neglect an area in your life that you perhaps don't feel comfortable with or don't have as much clarity around. You don't have the boundaries. You use the inherent boundaries of the workplace environment to avoid setting boundaries or establishing boundaries in other areas of life. We know there's a paycheck, we know there's a need that's met. We know there's a validation, we know there's a role, whereas maybe at home, those things aren't as clear. We have to do that work with ourselves.

In a famous Zen story, a monk carries a woman across a puddle; however, as ascetics they're not permitted to touch women. The one monk carries the woman across the puddle, and about twenty minutes after they crossed the other monk said, "Well, you carried that woman and you're not allowed."

He said, "Yeah, I let her go twenty minutes ago, and you're still carrying her."

Thoughts are what are greedy, not the physical act of doing something. The monk who didn't touch the woman was the one who was greedy and couldn't let go of the thoughts. The moment you have the thought, it already materializes, it already enters the body. It already enters your community; it already enters the world. The monk who never touched the woman carried the woman way longer and further than the monk that touched her and let her go. The minute you set boundaries, you're clear; you have values, you have limitations. You process the thought, emotion and desire. You let it go. You're not in this greed process of hoarding thoughts, emotions and desires that are linked to childhood that you don't want to let go of. Ralph Waldo Emerson stated "finish every day and be done with it, for manners and for wise living it is a vice to remember." Holding on to thoughts and emotions is greedy, it's a vice.

*The tarot card **The Tower**, representing chaos and falseness crumbling as to seek truth on a new solid foundation.*

Spiritual Striptease

In the tarot deck, the Tower card represents all falseness that needs to be broken, needs to collapse, needs to shatter. It's a very intense card. The *Ayin* is a Hebrew letter which means eyes. In order to see the truth, you need to remove the veils of illusion, what I call a spiritual striptease, to see the truth of yourself.

The sixteenth letter in the Hebrew alphabet, Ayin, meaning eyes. It also means the primeval light, the light of God. It indicates seeing your true source of light and removing the veils, the form covers you in, to not see the truth of your essence. In Kabballah philosophy it means nothingness, before the universe was created and wisdom comes into being from this nothingness. Again, spirit manifest into form.

When you start seeing the truth of yourself and removing the veils, you must set values. To live in truth, you need a philosophy of life. The number one thing about greed is not defining values, that's why it's greedy. Not wanting to have any definition, any boundaries, any limits, and pretending that you're omnipotent and divine when you're in a limited body, is narcissistic and greedy. You can apply this to your own life. I ask clients, "What are your top two values?" (and it cannot be family). Once they answer, often generically like integrity and honesty, they must define the generic values in a minimum of three observable and measurable terms to back up the definition. This is the only way to set a boundary on the subconscious, stop self-betrayal and hold ourselves accountable.

When I asked Jacqueline during a session what her top value was, she answered "Honesty," but she couldn't define it. She shared a story about her workplace. Being a manager, she directs and guides her colleagues; however, her version of this is to say "I'm going to give you a loving suggestion." This is covert power and manipulation. An employee who receives this type of guidance doesn't know how to succeed. They're being set up for failure. There's no clarity in this comment and there's no structure or definable, measurable objectives for this employee to succeed. In an attempt to make others feel comfortable, we avoid the discomfort of clarity. Jacqueline decided that her first measurable directive for honesty would be to give a clear directive, an actionable item. When an employee has a bad idea, she would clearly state "throw that in the garbage it's a bad idea". There's an observable and measurable directive. Holding yourself and others accountable may not be nice, but it is kind and truthful. This is adulting and this is not self-betrayal; this is self-love.

Morgan Freeman played God in the movie *Bruce Almighty* and he said, "I am God, so it's easy to play him." There's a divine spark in the world expressed only through you, but you need to be in the body so the spark can shine. Illness is often the only way we may know how to keep our God complex or narcissism in check. One of the reasons we create illness is to return to the humbleness of the form, the body, and recognize we're just human and common like everyone else.

Pride was the deadliest of sins according to Greek values. Narcissism is directly linked to pride, and it's difficult to balance since we are all divine. Judgments play a role because they're linked to our value system. I say, judgements are confessions and they're great! Without judgements we wouldn't know what our bad bucket or shadow values are that are stored in the subconscious and projected onto others. We have shadow or bad bucket values that are linked to the deadly sins, vices or passions, and good bucket values or values like integrity, honesty and loyalty to counteract and balance out the bad bucket values. Bad bucket values pose a problem. We believe that because we have these values, we are bad people. It's actually trying to hide these shadow aspects of ourselves that builds our narcissism and gets us sick. Be honest about your bad bucket values. We all have them, and they lead us to our true selves when we own these unintegrated aspects of ourselves. If we hide behind only the good bucket values, and fail to properly define these, we cannot become whole, and rather, become sick.

Recently, Google decided they wanted to change their interview and hiring process and they said they wanted somebody who is humble and argues. They said that successful bright people rarely experience failure, so they don't learn how to learn from the failure. They instead commit the fundamental attribution error, which is if something good happens, it's because they're a genius, and if something bad happens, it's someone else's fault. This is what we cannot do; that's greedy. *It's never me, it's never me, it's always the other person.* That's a very covert power currency of manipulation. What did Google do? They decided that they wanted people that argue for their point of view. That's your value system. You know what your values are so clearly, that you're willing in a meeting or on a project to argue and fight for your value system. In the same light, you're humble enough to know when you don't know something or when you're wrong.

Laszlo Bock, Google's former Senior Vice President of People Operations, says you need a big ego and a small ego in the same person at the same time. This is the gift of Saturn. This is the limitation; this is using work as sacred space. This is using the body, discernment, and the work environment, to monitor your narcissism and your ego. Be humble enough to know when you're wrong or to listen to the other person. This is indeed a real leader.

Limitations and Boundaries

Saturn is also known as the god Cronos. He represents chronological time and he oversees our work and professional life. He's the one that teaches us to conform, to bend, to be supple, to be flexible. We need some time with the seven-year cycles of the skinny cows of Saturn so that we can grow into who we need to be. He oftentimes resembles Scrooge, why? Because Scrooge was greedy, depressed, angry, and bitter. If you do not use your work environment to become flexible, supple, and move with the rhythm of the seasons, the changes in your work experience, in your work life, you're going to break if you don't bend, because you're dry and bitter. High vibration Saturn is not greed—it's actually limitations and boundaries. Selfish is if you take someone's power or they take yours. Self is when you own your power, and you don't take anybody else's. Saturn is the right way to teach Self.

Having limits is not being greedy, saying no is not being greedy. Me not giving you the real estate in my head is not being greedy, it is self-love; it is authenticity. When you start defining your values, you can become authentic. This is the template for your behavior. Then you can show up as the authority, as the king, as the ruler that Saturn in the highest vibration represents. It is practically impossible to find someone who knows their values, sets their limits, and owns their power. It is rare to find someone like that, like a unicorn. Saturn the planet has rings around; its rings limit you. It gives you boundaries, your values are defined.

Your parents gave you a value system upon conception, you do not change from that value system. What you do is, in a passive-aggressive covert power currency, you manipulate by saying you're one thing when really, you're honoring their system. Because you don't ever want to question and dethrone them—again, greedy, wanting it all. Your mom and dad will always serve as counsel. They live in your head. In the sixth chakra, there are two lotus petals. One represents mother and the other father. They are the voices in your head, and should be metaphorically consulted with, but it is your kingdom so make the values they imparted on you, your own. There are going to be limitations; every person, place, thing, or situation is mother or father for a reason. Because in this life, in this vibration, in this consciousness, you came to have them as a template, but you use that template to then clearly define your own values.

The ajna chakra, sixth chakra or third eye is located in the center of the forehead, between the eyebrows, in the energetic body, not the physical body. Depicted with two lotus petals on either side, one representing the masculine principle and the other representing the feminine principle. The center circle represents the void, or the throne, each individual must assume upon reaching balance in the energy body. The downward triangle represents the ethereal being found in the feminine polarities in the body. The OM symbol represents the bija or seed mantra, the sound that resonates with this chakra.

In your sixth chakra, in your kingdom (the throne in your head), you need the "gods" to have given you a template. Those gods are mom and dad; you cannot defy them. It's about dethroning them and using what they taught you. That template doesn't harm you, but rather helps you. Saturn is conformity and conforming; however, not blindly. Rather with strong values and boundaries that gives your psyche structure and your life meaning.

Horai, the goddesses in Greek mythology are known as *Dike, Eunomia and Irene*. These three represent Horai, the Greek word for time or seasons. Everything has a season. Dike is justice. Justice is served. Release the outcome. The Universe will take care of that. You are not God; you do not have access to the outcome of every situation. You trying to control it is very material and greedy; we need order. The seasons have an order. Eunomia is good order, we know that every winter is followed by spring. We see this; it is trustworthy and security that we can count on. Irene is wealth and peace. It's not greedy to be adaptable, it's not greedy to have both power currencies, it's not greedy to set limits and boundaries. It's actually going to give you peace and wealth, both spiritual and material.

Mirrors

Leaders need mirrors. The person that you hate at work is most like you, and you don't want to see it. If you define your values clearly, you will start seeing it. The ones you don't like are the ones you need to work through, because it's something in yourself that needs adaptability. You're up against the clock, so to speak, because Chronos or Saturn is time, and you will die eventually. During the course of your work span, your workday, your work lifetime or your entire lifetime, you're going to be "produced." The people that mirror back to you things that you need to work on are part of your backstage assistance team. Use them as mirrors. Sometimes you're going to be the main star; maybe at work you're the CEO. Maybe at home you know your partner is the main star. There are times for being in front, very overt, and times for being back, very covert. A king needs counsel, and leaders need mirrors. We do not do anything alone; you cannot be overt all the time or covert all the time. We actually do need mirrors. The judgments we have about others, help us see ourselves more clearly. What we don't like in others, is simply what we dislike in ourselves and have failed to integrate. There is no hierarchy in the spirit realm, we need to be team players and leaders simultaneously. There are two leadership styles. The traditional leader where the leaders at the top and then the servant leader were the leaders at the bottom. I prefer a cyclical leadership style where everyone's needs are met, my Self as Service model and what I call my *Chocolate Chip Cookie Theory of Leadership.*

The "Chocolate Chip Cookie Theory of Leadership"

The "Chocolate Chip Cookie Theory of Leadership" is based on my theory that the Universe is symbolic of an entire batch of cookie dough. Imagine a roll of Nestle Toll House cookie dough. You, the individual soul and body, are just a "plop" on the cookie sheet. On your cookie sheet, there are two halves. Your half, with your chocolate chip, is your throne. On the other side of the sheet are eleven mini chocolate chips. In total these 12 chocoalte chips represent (metaphorically) the 12 Olympian gods or the 12 archetypes found in the office.

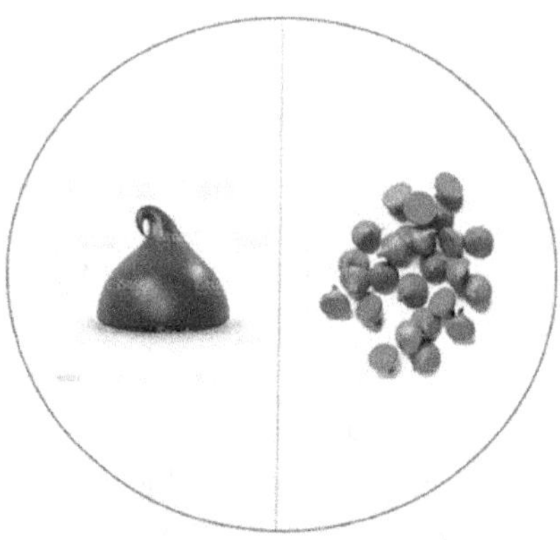

The Chocolate Chip Theory of Leadership *represents you, your solar energy and rational principle on the left as one intact chocolate chip. On the right, eleven chocolate chips, representing the eleven archetypes found in your colleagues, that mirror you, as to show you what needs to be integrated. Wholeness is found within when all twelve archetypes are working in unison in the psyche.*

Our main chocolate chip represents ourselves, the sun or hero archetype in our life; however, the eleven chocolate chips on the right represent the remaining planetary archetypes in our head that become the team we work with, what is left to integrate in ourselves to be whole. You cannot look at the sun directly; to avoid getting blinded, you must look around the sun, towards the shadow. The eleven chocolate chips, opposite your large chocolate chip are the shadow aspects of yourself, which you cannot see, but which your team mirrors back for you so you can grow. We think that we're judging the lazy guy in the cubicle, the dirty girl down the street, the one who talks loud in meetings; we think that it has nothing to show us. In your life, you're the authority. Using work as a sacred space and using these archetypes as mirrors helps you show up as the authority of your life, no matter the situation.

The Theme of Twelve

In Greek philosophy, the *dodekatheism* are worship of the twelve Olympian gods. There are twelve disciples in the Bible, and there are twelve archetypes in our psyche that I refer to as the psychological organs. They're all saying the same thing: these are aspects of your mind, they show up, and what we want to do is get them in congruence. You show up as one divine person, one whole individual, not fragmented. The roles determine who you're going to be and where you're going to show up. Your value system, your philosophy of life, and your rulebook is going to determine that. If you know all twelve archetypes are in you and everything is a mirror, like in the Chocolate Chip Leadership Theory, then every single archetype is going to show you what you need to integrate.

At the Last Supper with Christ were his disciples, and Zeus led the other eleven Olympians. Twelve is a theme. Imagine eleven employees gathered around a conference table. Assume that these disciples, Olympians or archetypes are your fellow employees, bosses or leaders. The chocolate chips don't have to have any religious significance; it's simply aspects of your mind. There are twelve archetypes, and we have all of these in our psyche. We represent the solar achetype, the other eleven chocolate chips represent our shadow aspects. Together we represent the twelve archetypes or Olympian gods, that are found in our psyche. Integration of the twelve, make us whole and individuated.

We show up in different ways. Your rational nature is the sun or your solar archetype. This is how you see yourself and how you show up at the workplace. However, the other eleven are also aspects of yourself, you may not easily see, but others do see and represent back to you as a mirror. Your emotional nature is the moon, your intellectual nature is Mercury. Think of the people in your work that meet these criteria. You've got maybe the aggressive or angry archetype in Mars. The loving, compassionate or sensual archetype in Venus. Jupiter may be the loud person, that traveler or the know-it-all. You've got Saturn, maybe more of the depressed, limited person, or the old, wise person. Uranus is the chaotic, rebellious and irreverent one, and Pluto is the heavy, silent type who may be very jealous, possessive, or envious. Neptune is innocent-like or flaky. Chiron is maybe someone who's very sick or acts like the wounded warrior. The scandalous or the vulgar employee is the Black Moon Lilith. All of these archetypes are in your psyche and in your workplace, reflecting all the shadow aspects of yourself that you cannot see when directly looking at the sun, yourself.

In the Bible story of Joseph, he saw eleven stalks of wheat bow to him in the center as the sun. This story is a metaphor for you, your psyche, your archetypes and the players in your workplace. These archetypes are there to help you mirror yourself, to bow to you so that you could see where you need to bow down and bend. Bend and integrate your values, your rulebook and your philosophy of life.

The eleven archetypes that are represented by shadow aspects in colleagues, bosses and those that mirror you. They are expressed here by the astrological planetary glyphs. In the center is the sun glyph or solar aspect of self. All twelve archetypes are found in your psyche and mirrored by everyone in your life. All twelve archetypes have low vibration consciousness linked to vices as well as high vibration consciousness linked to the virtues. Wholeness is dependent on balancing both the lower and higher consciousness of each archetype.

The heart chakra is representative of wholeness. Once we have integrated all of the archetypes, we then return back to the heart and begin our service to others. This is the Self as Service model. You cannot serve, truthfully without having individuated, owned all shadow aspects (chocolate chips) of Self, otherwise the service is simply to cover up shadow aspects and vices. Each chakra, located in the energy body, has a certain number of lotus petals. There are twelve petals in the heart chakra, one for each archetype in the psyche that must be integrated for you to become whole and individuated, this then leads to agape love, service to another. Once integrated, then you can open your heart space for others. Like Hercules in the eleventh labor, you can begin loving another and serve a higher calling. You must integrate each archetype, become whole, and then you can live a heart-centered life. The heart is the highest vibration of Virgo, which is another theme of the sixth house, service. There's no hierarchy in the universe, so in my model of leadership, it's about team building, being a leader and a team player at the same time. My leadership model is circular, indicating spirituality and the universal hierarchy, which is that we are all one; we serve ourselves and serve others, equally.

The heart or anahata chakra, associated with love, compassion and joy. It has twelve lotus petals.and represents the union of male and female as well as the universal consciousness and the earthly consciousness. The twelve petals are linked to spiritual ignorances and spiritual developments, as humans encompass both to be whole. The heart chakra represents a limited bounded sense of self, but with the process of discrimination between vice and virtue, both are needed for wholeness.

My twelve values for leadership on my leadership wheel mentioned earlier, and included here once again are: 1) Vision, 2) Dedication, 3) Adaptability, 4) Empathy, 5) Authenticity, 6) Service, 7) Honesty, 8) Influence, 9) Integrity, 10) Respect, 11) Resilience, and 12) Personal Development. These are the themes that I, as a leader, as well as a team player, need to provide or participate in. I go more in depth to this leadership wheel in Chapter Seven.

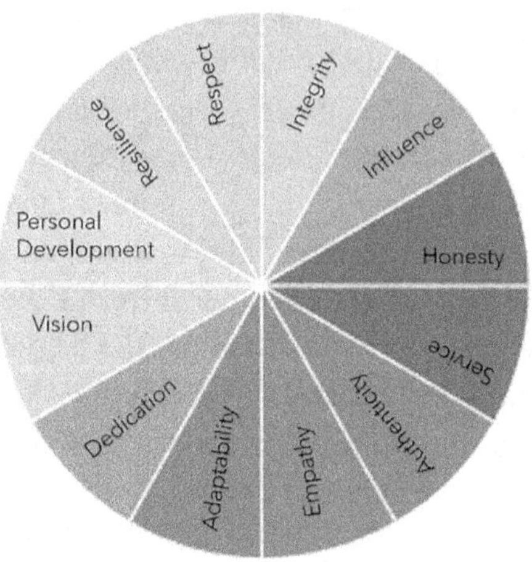

The Leadership Wheel representing the twelve values of leadership.

CHAPTER 6
Dethroning the CEO and COO

This is Nathaniel, my narcissistic cookie. I purchased him on Etsy and named him Nathaniel because it means "given by God". My divine spark, as well as my warts and shadow aspects are all representations of the divine. It is my job to integrate both divine and human aspects in my work. This is also a reminder that I am not the entirety of the universal cookie dough, as a narcissistic would believe to be, but rather just a small portion.

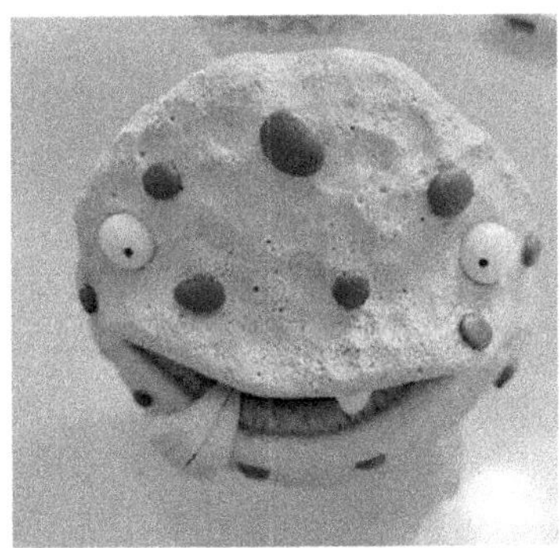

Nathaniel, the narcissistic cookie, a symbol used as a reminder that I am divine and human. His chocolate chips indicate I am all of the aspects found in others as well.

As a leader and a team player, you're going to make mistakes; therefore, I use this cookie as a reminder to love myself, warts and all. This is one example of how a leader needs a mirror. Use the workspace to develop self-love qualities, and use the people in your work environment to learn and grow. The cookie reminds me to go through my personal TED talk when a judgement arises, to remind myself that the judgement is about myself, and it becomes much easier to let it go and resolves 90 percent of the conflict in a few short seconds.

The Universe responds to your state of mind as a mental projection. You are an aspect of this universal space; therefore, it is your job to show off your cookie dough, to find a way to express your divinity through your humanity, your body. The personal TED talk is to remind yourself to ask three questions immediately upon conflict entering your sphere of consciousness. All conflict is an attempt at self-love; however, based on previous childhood programming, what we inevitably end up doing is returning to a child script and repeating what our parents taught us about ourselves, limited love and needs, and that's how we typically show up for ourselves. If we TED talk a conflict situation, we can diffuse the determined response and actually pause and take a breath, choosing for ourselves rather than basing our actions on a predetermined behavioral response dictated by our parents.

If you're not aware of your programming, then it's difficult to show up for yourself; therefore, the TED talk brings you to the present moment and reminds you that the conflict is internal and the situation is mirroring your own psyche. When a colleague or a supervisor annoys you, you will have an impure thought: *"I don't like you. You're annoying. I'm smarter than you."* What we allow into our sphere of consciousness is intentional, so it is a mirror you created to grow. Impure thoughts or judgements never go away. We are conceived on an impure thought. That thought enters your consciousness level immediately when you're engaging with another person, especially at work. So if you can identify it through a split-second TED talk and let it go, then you can be present for what's showing up in your consciousness to help you grow. So when I stop to talk to someone at work, I am choosing this moment. I am choosing very intentionally that I'm allowing this situation into my sphere of consciousness. I'm allowing this in because there's something for me to learn from it. According to Saturn, I will be involved in some workspace for thirty years minimum; I want to make it work for me.

In Greek, the word *eudaimonia* translates as a state of good spirit, happiness or contentment. Something spoken about in philosophy is that virtues are states of the soul: welfare, human flourishing, and prosperity are all the determinants of happiness and contentment, more so than achieving financial prosperity or whatnot; these are things of the soul. That's why this book is all about using the workplace to do your dharma. The workplace is the space where you can really exercise your own leadership in your own life.

My wheel of integrative or cyclical leadership is to lead you to dethroning your CEO and COO. Your CEO is your Chief Enlightenment and Chief Energetic Officer, and your COO is your Chief Ordinary Officer and Chief Originality Officer. A Chief Enlightenment Officer is linked to spirit and how we can show up in the workplace working on our spirit. The Chief Energetic officer is more of the material aspect: it's the money, and the resource is time and energy.

My client Dick used verbiage like reimagining, refashioning, recrafting, repackaging repeatedly during a session. In his psyche, he was convincing himself that he was taking someone else's content and repackaging it differently and calling it original, however, when we deconstructed the conflict, he realized there wasn't a lot of originality to what he was doing. According to my concept that there are no new stories, we are all in essence repackaging old myths and living them, but in our own divine way. However, Dick wasn't living out his myth, he was living someone else's by not creating new and original content through his business, and it had been affecting his health. His use of archetypal language made it clear that he was afraid of being unoriginal. One of the biggest fears that I hear in practice is a fear of being ordinary. Archetypally, Uranus rules originality, freedom, and eccentricity, and Saturn rules limitations, rules, boundaries and ordinary day-to-day activities; however, it is the midpoint of these two that we aspire to achieve wholeness and balance.

I attended the van Gogh immersion experience in Miami and learned that van Gogh's last work was called *Tree Roots*. Roots, metaphorically, indicate Saturn, groundedness, being in the body; however, van Gogh's whole modus operandi was the tortured soul, the Uranus archetype, the artist who chopped off his ear and was placed in an insane asylum. Upon van Gogh discovering his ordinariness, noted by his physician and then his work *Tree Roots*, he committed suicide. Ordinariness, without the originality to balance it, can lead to boredom, depression, anxiety, and an unlived life.

Many people wish to be original, so that instead, they create chaos as the way they show up in the world, in an attempt at individuality, creativity and originality. It is the same archetype, but a very different vibration. Upon creating chaos, and whatever backlash you receive, you can immediately enter the psychological orgasm by confirming the impure thought and judgement you wanted to prove from childhood. Wherever your point of entry is to the chaos, when you're proven correctly, *"I knew I was a loser," "Oh, I knew I was going to get hurt,"* or *"Oh, I knew she was going to dump me."* Whatever your gas releases in the system, you get an orgasm from proving yourself correctly. This is the vicious cycle of chaos in an attempt to be original. All the chaos is an attempt to not be ordinary. van Gogh's last masterpiece is roots! It's almost like he had this moment of, *"Oh my god, I'm just ordinary. I'm just an ordinary human, I can't live."*

Uranus in our psyche, at a low state of consciousness, creates chaos as a way of being different. When you think, *"I'm so different,"* you're not, you're just chaotic. When we start realizing that chaos is another word for the archetype of originality, we realize that we haven't really identified how to be original, and that's why we're creating all this chaos in our life. Through our work experience, we can find that midpoint between originality and ordinariness between the originality, which is our divine spark, and our ordinariness of being human.

Finding where that midpoint is at really is a big function of your life. So you're the COO of your life in this discovery process. The CEO, the enlightenment, is the divinity of how you're going to use experiences mirrored at you by the chocolate chips on your team to learn and grow. If you allowed it into your sphere of consciousness, then this means that there's something for you to learn. If I'm allowing something to enter my space, if I create everything, then there's something in this for me. At this point, my ears perk up, and I can become *"enlightened"* from this person, document, or email. I never miss a beat in the attempt at enlightenment.

How you use your energy is directly related to your self-worth. What's your energy currency at work? Your money. How much you get paid; what you get as per the service that you provide. So how to manage your money is also linked to your time or resources. Because it's not just financial money that is the energetic component to you being the CEO of your life. Here you see that at work, you get to show up as the leader all the time. I call it the Chairman of the Hoard. Indeed, be greedy in this sense, make it all about you, because it is. Once you establish this, then you can give back.

Kierkegaard talks about free will and freedom as a big nothing. He states that humans are contrary creatures, thinking they want freedom from all constraints, yet, they are terrified of freedom. The whole point of life, and our work lives, is to learn the balance between the spirit and matter. Our rational minds and intellectual capacity should balance our intuitive spiritual connection to the Universal cookie dough; living as one, as unified consciousness. Kierkegaard says the best place to become divine and human is through the experience in our work world. So at work we can unite ourselves in both a spiritual and a material manner.

Charles runs a spiritual business and educational center; however, just because your business is of a spiritual nature, does not mean you're involved in spiritual activities or doing spiritual inner work. We somehow think that if it's packaged as spirit, then it's spirit. For some reason, we think if we're in a spiritual environment, the mere fact of being in a spiritual space, doesn't mean we're doing spiritual work. Spiritual work is shadow work, a deeper reflection of our impurest natures and finding the divinity in ourselves, despite these flaws. Spiritual work is inner work. It's understanding your thoughts, your emotions, your desires. This is why work is such the place where we grow and learn and it doesn't matter the industry you're in. It's what you glean from that work environment for your self-improvement. It does not matter what industry you're in—if you're in mechanics, if you're in finance. Spirituality is the inner space.

Saint Thomas Aquinas said, "Peace implied a two-fold union; the result of one's own appetite being directed to one object." That's the purpose of the personal TED talk: if you're at work or you're in a situation and you have the thought, the impure thought, *"I'm better than this person,"* you work through that, and then once you identify the thought is about yourself, you can let that go. You've now taken that thought and it no longer penetrates the real estate in your mind. You let it go, then there's space!

What he's calling peace or *eudaimonia*, welfare or contentment is the twofold process or the twofold union. It's one's own appetite being united with an appetite of another. Jupiter and Venus archetypes represent your spiritual journey, but also a material one as well. The CEO is linked to the Jupiter and the Venus archetypes. It's not just spiritual growth. It is linked to your spiritual and your financial worth. This is the part of you that's the CEO, managing your energy appropriately, and where the COO unites as both the originality and the ordinariness. *Mind Your Pleck* is a concept I picked up when I was in Amsterdam. The airport had stations that said "mind your pleck." I asked a friend, and she said it meant "mind your place and mind your things" at the airport. This can be extrapolated to life. The way you manage your time, money and resources—your things, speaks to knowing your place or your self-worth. So when Saint Thomas says this about peace being twofold, the Venus archetype represents the circle of spirit, and the cross of matter. We need both to be balanced. Kings need counsel, and if you see yourself as the king or the CEO of your life, you are always going to have eleven chocolate chips, the archetypes, disciples or Olympians as a mirror to you archetypically in your workplace. You're always literally the king of your life; it's your throne. But that council is always around you. The objective is for you to become the leader of your own life using the work environment.

The glyph of Venus, representing the circle of spirit, our divinity and the cross of matter, our humanity and desirous body.

Use these experiences for your growth—spiritual and financial, rather than letting them burn you out and make you stressed or sick. Aristotle said that the goal, eudaimonia, was human flourishing and the highest human good. What is the best way you can show up? If you have this attitude that you make space for the other, then you can really start living from that space of the highest good, but not at your own expense. Aristotle said the highest good of a thing consists of the good performance of its characteristic function. The virtue or excellence of a thing consists of whatever traits or qualities enable it to perform that function well. There's an example of a knife: a knife's main function or highest function is to cut. If you're not living from your originality, if you're not living from this enlightened, highest state, your originality or divine spark, then you haven't fulfilled your function.

Sandy, a client who works in graphic design, speaks frequently of hierarchy and design. When she teaches the students to layout a website, for instance, there's an ordinariness to the order you're going to follow with your eye to draw the viewer in; however, as you layer color, fonts and the design elements that give the personality or originality of the design, it all ties together. It's the same metaphor in our work life.

Yes, there's hierarchy, there is leadership, there is a chain of command. But then there's something that's woven hopefully throughout the entire organization that should be the mission, the vision, and the value system. It ties the entire organization together, making it original, despite the ordinariness of its structure and even perhaps the end objective of, for instance, selling widgets. In order to be the CEO and COO of your life, you must know the hierarchy in your life—whether it's your family or the position you hold at work. How do you tie in those other elements to make it original?

Whole Person Leadership

There is a movement now called *whole person leadership*. Jeff Bezos said that work-life balance is actually a debilitating term. A lot of the literature written about this whole person leadership has to do with a mindset of growth, at the same time as having self-reflection and introspection. Again, it's the spirit and the matter. Yes, we have competition, we have goals, we've got metrics that we have to abide by and gain financially, but there's room for the whole person to grow. Bezos and others are saying that this whole person leadership, which is similar to my chocolate chip model, is that in addition to perhaps the financial or the material goals, that the goals have introspection. Inner growth as a result of that external growth—and that piece has been missing from leadership, from our lives, from work culture for a very long time. If it's not incorporated into the culture, my proposition for you is that this becomes the culture in which you create in the organization so that people understand that spiritual work in whatever industry you're in is possible. So they don't waste these years and feel empty upon retirement because their spiritual life has been voided. Rather, they understand that every situation, anything that's allowed into the sphere of consciousness, is an opportunity for raising consciousness. Whole life leaders lead from their authentic inner core to become the leader they desire to be.

How do you become the CEO and the COO of your life and live authentically? You need to have a vision, you need to have a mission, and you need to have core values. Organizations should have a vision statement. The vision statement should be huge; it should be something global, all-inclusive.

The Warby Parker vision is **affordable eye care for everybody**. Tom's Shoes' is **everybody has shoes, nobody is barefoot or has no footwear**. These are very global initiatives. The vision statement for my life is to eliminate spiritual coercion. These are supposed to be larger-than-life goals! There has to be a vision for your life in order for you to be an authentic leader in your own life. Again, this has nothing to do with leading groups. If you happen to be in a leadership position, perfect: it's going to be applicable. But, it's about being the leader, so that you gain your authentic inner self. If truly worked through, you are served and you're serving others. That's true contentment and balance.

Your mission is linked to your material or your business perspective, maybe your earthly needs. My mission statement is **to use universal laws for modern-day application**; this will guide my earthly resources, like what my offerings will be and how often. Whereas the vision is more of your spiritual needs or your spiritual desires at a very global high impactful state of being. The way you're going to get there is through your values. List your top two values (can't be family) in definable, measurable terms, no less than three criteria each.

My mission is accomplished through spiritual education and counseling, so that's how I'm going to make money. My mission and how I'm going to make money is very clear: you pay me for a session; I get paid, I establish my mission. Check. Now, my vision is I want to free people from spiritual coercion whether it's gurus or teachers or churches or cults, because my life led me to this career path via that exact problem, that wound. Usually when you're doing your vision statement for your life, that would then hopefully align with the vision statement of your job. That's the whole purpose! You have to identify what global mission you'd be interested in achieving in the world. I'm not going to free everybody from coercive techniques. Obviously it's supposed to be huge; it's supposed to be larger than life. It's supposed to be a purpose-driven identity that you have so that you have the will to keep going and serving others.

Your values should tie into both the vision and the mission. My top two values are spirituality and leadership. Spiritual leadership is what I hope to evoke as a result of client connections and student connections. This is of course linked to my vision, which is releasing people of spiritual coercion from cults, religion, teachers, and gurus so they can become self-reliant on their own spiritual inner core values. It all ties together. This is how the organization that you work for should technically operate, as should your life.

Hieros Gamos

The *hieros gamos* is a term for a mystical marriage, the metaphor is used to represent the marriage between your spiritual and material consciousness, your masculine and feminine aspects, your shadow and light as well as your work life and your personal life. The *Vesica Pisces* below is used to name the two interrelating circles, your spirit and your matter. In the workbook section, you will use this model to identify your mission, vision, non-negotiable, unmet need and thread of how your spiritual and material lives overlap. Place the vision and the mission of the organization you work for under matter, and your vision and mission for your life under spirit. The overlapping oval is called the mandorla and links to the thread of why you have that job, a nonnegotiable and unmet need. The marriage of the spirit and the matter. There should be one thread tying you to that job in terms of the material world—let's say a paycheck, mentoring, learning leadership skills.

Next, identify the one nonnegotiable that breaks the contract because you will not self betray (ie., asked to cook the books) and one unmet need you will get fulfilled as a part of this organization (ie, validation with each employee evaluation or annual bonus). These items should correlate to your life's vision and mission as well.

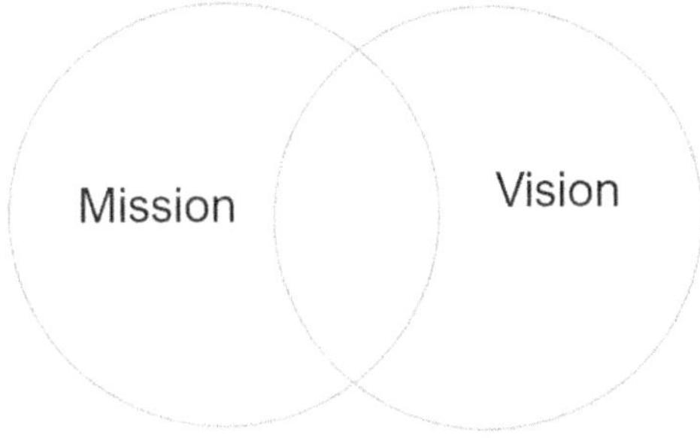

The Vesica Pisces sacred geometry symbol to identify the mission and vision of the organization and your life, and where they overlap, to serve your material needs and spiritual needs, simultaneously.

PERMA

Martin Seligman, a psychologist and the founder of the Positive Psychology Center at the University of Pennsylvania, uses the acronym PERMA: Positive Emotion, Engagement Relationships, Meaning and Accomplishments for his theory on well-being. He states that well-being is established over time with these five elements; this leads to eudaemonia, what I call *workplace wellness*. Workplace wellness is not a meditation center down the hall or a gym or lunchroom stocked with organic juices. Workplace wellness is showing up as a whole person, your *hieros gamos*, working on both your spiritual and your material selves; working on your energy; working on your ordinariness and your originality; living out your vision, your mission and of course your core values, while at work. He says positive emotion, engagement, relationships, meaning, and accomplishment are all part of being or measuring well-being. If we're looking at it from the eudaemonia perspective, that's what he's saying would achieve workplace wellness.

Bill Parcells, a head coach in the NFL for nineteen seasons, called an ordinary player a JAG, *Just Another Guy*. Basically, a JAG was a player that didn't really have any superior outstanding qualities. Many clients struggle with a JAG mentality in the business sector, it's the ordinary aspect they struggle with, because without a clear vision, mission and values, you cannot find the originality. What makes you original? What is it that only you can bring to the table?

Stone Soup

An activity I use with clients, called *Stone Soup*, is to help you identify the wound, which is where your originality lies. During our zero to seven years, we have a wound created at a moment, big or small, where our psyche identified it wasn't fully accepted by the parents exactly as we were. At seven, our snow globe shatters and in our childhood something happens. That wound becomes our identity that is woven through every story that we tell. Some wounds are very subtle, but it is woven in what they speak.

Stone Soup is a child's book written by Ann McGovern in 1968. In a nutshell, a foreigner comes to town with an empty cooking pot and starts boiling a stone. One villager is curious and asks, "What are you doing?"

He answers, "I'm making stone soup."

And one of the townspeople says, "I have carrots."

The foreigner says, "Bring it."

The other town folks say, "I have celery," "I have a potato." Suddenly, all the resources of everybody combined makes a soup. The stone was obviously a placeholder. That's us! We are an ingredient, a supremely important ingredient. This is our originality that only we can bring. Maybe your vegetable is just one, but it's you, and the way you bring that to the workforce, to your family, to your team is what makes you so special. And it's the originality that only you can bring. So in the end of the story, everybody was nourished, everybody was fed. And that's a very important thing about workplace wellness. Are you being fed, and are you feeding others?

In the *Stone Soup* assignment I give clients, I tell them to write out all your memories or all your stories on small pieces of paper. Start at the youngest age possible. Write out the big, broad strokes of your life; write down keywords on a piece of paper. Then put them in a circle, like a soup, and take a picture. Now you have your stone soup: that circle tells you your wound, that circle shows you the thread woven through. It's like a life's resume. So, if you start seeing sexual assault or harassment, poverty or, in my case, spiritual coercion, you can identify the thread and the wound. I started seeing this in every single thing of my life. Obviously that led me to my vision. Spiritual coercion was the theme that I saw repeatedly. Even if you discover the thread of the soup is ordinary, you have an original take on it.

In my book *The Seven Gates: Seven Steps Beyond Self-Awareness,* I write of a client who kept dating women that had either been sexually abused or sexually assaulted, or she had friends that had been raped or sexually assaulted. She identified her vision to be larger than life. It was linked to some purpose, some vision or mission, of helping people, specifically women of a certain age group, with either history of sexual harassment or sexual assault. So our thread and our purpose, which becomes our vision, is directly related to our wound.

Instead of getting sick to create space for our spiritual lives, we can have workplace wellness, when we actually engage and find meaning in these threads rather than separating them, or worse, hiding them, as if they serve no purpose or they keep us different or ill. A big part of understanding the stone soup is that the wound, the thread, that you're viewing as negative, ill, keeps you different, abandoned or unlovable, is actually the vision and the purpose of your life. When you can see it from a global perspective, then you can get down to the mission.

Ikigai is a Japanese concept that gives a person a sense of purpose. It's a series of overlapping circles that asks things like *what are you good at, what do you love, what does the world need, and what can you be paid for?* It's a similar idea to *Stone Soup.* Service leadership, I believe, takes away from workplace wellness. I think it links to burnout. Service over self is not genuine or in balance, it's self as service that creates wellness.

There's this old proverb that says, *"If you want to go fast, go alone; but if you want to go far, go together."* That's very different than sacrificing yourself. Going fast is a Mars archetype rooted in competition and although necessary in the earthly realm, play is the language of spirit and inner work. Service leadership that's sacrificial is a Neptune archetype; however, the Venus archetype, on the other hand, promotes teamwork, going further—everyone wins. If your spiritual work has become competition, it's not spiritual work. If your dharma has become competitive, it's no longer a dharma.

In talking to a client recently, she was being competitive with her mothering between her and her ex-husband. I said, "You know your dharma gets lost in that competition." This idea of dharma being your duty, your spiritual duty so to speak, at whatever stage of life you are, and hers at that moment is mothering—if you're trying to compete, it's lost all of the dharma associated with it. The moment you attach competition and goal, that's it, it became material. Outcome wins, no matter pertaining to any industry, even your soul, are material wins of the earthly world. Process wins are spiritual wins. There's no earthly reward or validation, but your inner fire strengthens and you can sense the grace associated with it.

How much of that work do you now internalize, apply, use the universal laws, do a TED talk, show up as an student, do a striptease, really get down to the core of who you are, give back as a result? When there's metrics attached, it becomes competitive. The dharma or the spiritual nature of it is gone. The only exception to this rule is defining your value system in measurable terms and measurable objectives. You cannot be spiritual and not use an experience that enters your consciousness if you don't have a value system to check it against.

Somebody said to me the other day, and they were feeling guilty, "I walked by a homeless person and I didn't give anything and that makes me feel very bad." First, guilt is a placeholder emotion for something less socially acceptable; therefore when you find yourself feeling or saying you feel guilty check that with the truth of what you're thinking. If you do not process that thought, you're losing your power. In a circumstance like this you write values and have a rule book around what you believe is your responsibility, in alignment with your values, so you do not self betray. Have a philosophy of life around how you're going to help people in need on the street, if they're drunk or if they're drugged or if they're homeless. If you don't go home and write a rule around philanthropy, when you'll donate, when you won't donate, then you're not managing your energy and your impure thoughts, emotions and desires are running the show. There goes your CEO out the window. Just because it enters your space, don't be quick to rely upon conventional morality of what you should do. The concept of askesis represents building a spiritual muscle through self-discipline. These small moments on whether to donate a dollar, speak up at a meeting, say no to a party etc....are practices on how to manage your fire and energy so when large life decisions, appear you have built your spiritual muscle on how to manage without losing yourself to the impure thoughts and emotions of a situation.

Everything is spiritual when you go home to the drawing board and you write values around it. It has nothing to do with the packaging that it's in, if it's entered your consciousness, don't miss that opportunity.

Self as Service Leadership

Rather than service-instead-of-self leadership, I propose a Self As Service Leadership style—it serves you and the other, both matter and spirit. Transparent leadership is an attempted leadership style where you let your employees be very open and honest. Yet most people don't feel that they can do that; they don't feel that there's authenticity in leadership. In your own life, as the CEO and the COO of your own life, authenticity is important. When you're authentic, you make someone feel safe. We all have a safety need. It's the first need: safety and security. When you're authentic, when you're that sort of leader, when you're transparent, you're actually allowing people to feel safe. They feel that they can trust you, and that they can be open with you, because you're being open with them. I'm very honest with my clients. When they struggle with a thought, I look over at my narcissistic cookie dough, warts and all, and I'm right there with them. I'm authentic and open and honest about my own struggles with these thoughts and how I manage to let them go, so they have permission to do the same.

Be on the *board of deflectors and be a no-sayer*. Toxic positivity is seeping into our lives with honesty about our issues being left behind. Well-being includes positive emotions; however, it does not mean only being positive, does not mean never saying no. Be a no-sayer instead of a naysayer; be on the board of deflectors. Don't just say yes, yes, yes to everything. You can say no gracefully: "That doesn't fit in my schedule," "I don't have time for that," "I'm already invited on many projects," "Honestly I've overbooked myself this week."

Workplace wellness is saying, I know how to manage my energy, my time and my resources. That's the energetic component of the CEO. And that's material. You only have a certain amount of money, you only have a certain amount of time, and you only have a certain amount of resources or energy. If you don't know how to navigate your energy correctly, you're going to feel like your boundaries have been violated and that you've felt limited, or you don't feel healthy. And that can lead you to sickness. Oftentimes those without boundaries and a clear value system are plugged into the energy source of fight-or-flight. That energy resembles a match. It's a quit shot, but fizzles quickly. Overtime you will be drained and get sick. If you're connected to a power source of the third chakra, a steady fire of self-worth guided by boundaries and values, it's a torch. It keeps burning and keeps you strong and healthy.

Be a *no sayer* and be on the *board of deflectors*. There is no reason why you have to say yes to everything that you're invited on. Just like if something comes into your sphere of consciousness, like an email or a directive from your boss. You have a right to ask. Go back to your values. Is this the shared value system in your job? It's you and your employer. What is the thread? The thread may be a paycheck, or it may not. What's the thread between you and your business? Between you and your place of employment? You need to know why you're there. It's fine if it's material and it's just a paycheck. Not a problem.

The thread serves to always go back to your values. If that thread and your value system don't line up, you're going to self-betray, you're going to be frustrated, you're going to get sick, get burnout and be stressed. This is the nonnegotiable: this is about being a *no sayer*. What are they asking you to do? Did someone ask you to change a grade? Did somebody ask you to sign a paper that you're not supposed to sign because it's postdated and that's illegal? What is your limit to what you will do for that paycheck, for that thread? What if perhaps your job asks you to do something against your value system? You have to be a *no sayer*. You need a nonnegotiable to check your values against.

In your field, there are things that are absolute nonnegotiables. In counseling, you do not sleep with a client. There is a rule that before you date a client, you wait two years from their termination date. You need to know your scope of practice. You need to know the rules, and if you're in a field where someone is asking you to violate a nonnegotiable. You have to know your value system really clearly, to know why you're there and what you're doing, and how that opportunity is showing up in your life for you to show up for yourself. If you don't know your value system, you will self betray. We don't change at our core, but we learn to make better choices when a value system is in place.

When Aristotle writes about the highest good, he is not ignorant to our lowest nature; however, it is an invitation to choose the highest version of yourself. A rule book, a philosophy of life and a value system established boundaries to help you choose the highest good.

No is a very powerful word and you need to understand that if you want to be the CEO of your life, because you don't have unlimited amounts of energy. You have to be a no sayer. Be on the board of deflectors, and go no, I can't. This is your life, this is your time, your money, your resources. Value it, because nobody else is going to value it.

Claude Poncelet, a physicist and a shaman, says that power loss is a shamanic illness. The idea of power loss, your energetic currency, is material. It is a material currency even though it might seem spiritual because it's energy, it's actually matter. When you lose your power, it's usually because your boundaries were violated, meaning you weren't a no sayer. You didn't know how to say no and allowed someone to violate your boundaries. The other way you lose power, according to Poncelet, is when you sacrifice your own integrity to get your needs met. If getting your validation needs met are more important than your nonnegotiable, you are in self-betrayal and at a major power loss. Poncelet says, when we internalize limiting beliefs, we lose energy.

The third way that we lose our power, or we get sick and we have no workplace wellness, is by something called entanglement. This is when we take energy that is not our own. You will take someone else's energy. If you are inhibiting or prohibiting someone from learning something, fending for themselves, learning a skill, you are entangled with their energy. You're not letting them be the CEO of their life. You can be counsel, but you must let them be the king on their throne.

If someone is taking energy from you, we call that power loss and violating boundaries. It's another form of entanglement or enmeshment. We do this with people, we do this at jobs. One of the ways that we do this in our job is working more and longer hours. I'm not saying that there aren't times it is appropriate. But if you do it gratuitously, day in and day out, you're stealing that energy from other areas of your life, from yourself. You're entangled with that job. It can be an inanimate sort of thing that you're entangled with, and that steals your power. There is no health in that.

There are two types of companies: mission-driven and purpose-driven, as there are lives. Will you have a mission-driven life or a purpose-driven life? If you're going to be a mission-driven company, you're going to have a mission to make x number of dollars selling x number of products or services. If you're a purpose-driven company, you're going to have a bigger vision: something that is helping society, the community, the world. It's going to be more socially conscious. Again, because this is about ourselves and being the CEO of our own lives, we have to be both mission-driven and purpose-driven. The mission-driven life is the earthly world: we need a paycheck, you want a title, you want to be validated, you want the corner office, you want the nice car and the expense account. How do you use the mission of the job and the people that you work with to make your life purpose-driven? When hiring an employee, you cannot eliminate the unmet needs, the validation needs, the need for money, from the person. Just like you can't change their eye color, their brown hair or blue eyes, you can't change that. You have to accept the individual as they are and know that that's what you're hiring. If you're satisfied at work, not only materially or mission-driven, that you got your paycheck, but you did your service, you made friends, then you're going to give back universally. You're going to go back to the fourth chakra, the wellness, to give to the other. Your fourth chakra is the heart center and true giving. Prior to that, you were "giving" to get your needs met, not altruistically. Once you meet your own needs, then you can actually start being of service to the "other" (humanity). That's the true eudaemonia! That's the true contentment, the true happiness. It's the true high-value individual that we put out into the world that makes the society and the world a better place.

But your life must contain both your job and the way you approach your life. Your work has to be both mission-driven and purpose-driven. In the past, people used to stay in a job twenty or thirty years, retire, get a pension. We don't see that now. The research shows that people stay about five years in a job. It makes sense. That's a Saturn cycle; five to seven years of skinny cows; then they get bored. They either go back to school, or find a different industry. So these are serial job hoppers, and what happens is a lot of them are noncommittal because they don't know their value system. They don't really know why they're hopping job to job. You might say it's kind of like having relationships: you're attracting the same person with a different face. You might be in the same job repeatedly with a different name or a different location. Really, it's linked to the inability to define or the ineffectiveness of having a value system in your life.

Elena came to me for help about which new job offer she should take. The first offer appeared to be chaotic, disorganized, and had a lower salary. The second job offer was higher pay, seemingly more professional, yet, she realized it had an organizational structure that she'd never acclimate to. Her friends insisted she take the higher pay, but I dissented. I was on her board of deflectors. When she TED talked the two jobs, as both created some level of inner conflict, the first job was an internal thought process she was struggling with about herself, while the second job resembled her childhood, structures she'd never be able to change, and she would have reached a dead-end at the job. The first job was representing inner limiting beliefs and thoughts about herself that with continuous inner work, and the *Chocolate Chip Leadership Theory*, she could ultimately change, as they were false beliefs, not permanent infrastructure.

Do your resources and schedule or material consequences keep you from seeking something different or making you stay in your current job? How is the job contributing to the vision that you have for your life? How does your job contribute to your vision, your larger vision?

Enneagram to Track Work Cycles

The Fourth Way enneagram is a tool used by Armenian philosopher G.I. Gurdjieff to describe the universal law, the Law of Octaves. The word enneagram is comprised of two Greek words, *ennea* (nine) and *gramma* (a drawing). The symbol is the enneagram and can be used to track your role at an organization and your work lifecycle. When either starting a business of your own or identifying the role you will have in an organization, start with the 1 point and place the year the organization started on that point.

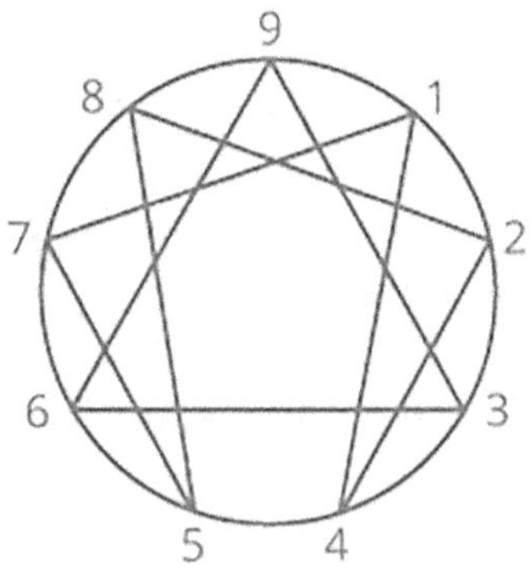

The Fourth Way enneagram, part of the esoteric system associated with Armenian philosopher Gurdjieff.

Follow the 1-9 sequence for each year it's been in operation. For instance, my previous employer opened, under a different name, in 1988. I started in 2004; therefore, the organization was in an eight year by the time I started. Staring with 1988 (1) and counting to 1996 (9), you begin again at (1) in 1997, and 2004 was an (8). My tenure started with an eight year, which means my role there was to be a position of power and money. I indeed was the Dean of Academics, and under my tutelage the campus grew to 500+ students, indicating more profits for the business. This also meant I gained more power in my life. Indeed, the schedule permitted me to have a thriving leadership position while still tending to my small children with a flexible schedule.

Each company has a lifecycle. Let me break down some basic keywords for each year below:

Year One: New Beginning
Year Two: Harmony & Conflict
Year Three: Communication
Year Four: Construction
Year Five: Growth
Year Six: Service, Health & Illness
Year Seven: Introspection
Year Eight: Power & Money
Year Nine: Endings, Downsizing

During a one year, you may get started, choose a name, get incorporated. In year two, you may have a conflict with purchasers or a coworker, or you may gain a business partner. Year three may increase your marketing budget so as to spread your message. During a four year, you may build a building or start planning your next launch or begin a rebrand to launch in year five. The five year is about growth: putting money into growing your company, personnel or marketing. Six years tend to be slow and steady years, about service, health and illness. It's also linked to the sixth house in astrology, and Virgo is the sixth sign. Seven years are introspective, so slowing down, regrouping, and downsizing is often accompanying the introspection. Seven years may feel like a values crisis or a spiritual crisis to the organization. Eight years bring the money, usually as a result of what newly constructed and implemented ideas occurred in years four and five. Nine years are closing cycles, so downsizing and recentering are common.

For instance, in 2021, Facebook began closing down Facebook and began promoting Meta. This was happening during a nine-year cycle as Zuckerberg prepared for the new one year, a new beginning. Facebook's previous nine year bottomed out in 2012, a typical nine-year cycle. Every organization has this lifecycle. Where you enter into that cycle speaks about your particular role in the organization. You can use this for being the CEO and the COO of your own life. If you're in a two role, one of your roles at the organization is to specifically build relationships. If you're in a three role, you may be there to make good friends or bring new ideas and a fresh perspective. In a four role, you're there for construction or conflict resolution. A five year is about growth and fun. Maybe you're hired as the party planner to student services. A six role is service, but also illness. During my six year at the university, I struggled with cancer and chemotherapy, so it became a focal point around my workspace, including creating a wellness center and breast cancer initiatives across campus. The enneagram helps you identify your role in that job, so that you know and you can go with that attitude. Does that link up to your thread, to your nonnegotiables, to your values, to your unmet needs? If you know your role based on the enneagram, you can go in with a different mindset and a clear boundary towards what you will achieve in both your material and spiritual life.

Shadow Aspects of the Enneagram

Each role has an energetic or emotional component. I'll list the themes below:

> Year One: Resentment & Anger
> Year Two: Flattery & Pride
> Year Three: Vanity & Deceit
> Year Four: Melancholy & Envy
> Year Five: Avarice & Greed
> Year Six: Cowardice & Fear
> Year Seven: Opportunism & Gluttony
> Year Eight: Vengeance & Lust
> Year Nine: Indolence & Sloth

Each of these roles have a vice or a "negative shadow" aspect that you can work on. If you're in a one role at work, one of the things that might develop that you can work through energetically is resentment.

In addition, you may have these shadow aspects based on your work year enneagram number.

> One: You are a leader; however, you may feel ambivalent because you feel separateness
>
> Two: You probably had protection needs and you fear getting close despite desiring harmony
>
> Three: You're the connector, but perhaps there is deceit, self-betrayal and manipulation
>
> Four: Four is a crisis number, so creating chaos, conflict and crisis creates a feeling of proximity to others here; you are trying, or you feel separated
>
> Five: You can show up as withdrawn and disconnected
>
> Six: Can be sick and have psychotic breaks, seeks validation
>
> Seven: These people can be loners, never seeking any workplace relationship
>
> Eight: This is someone who is power-hungry and will make shady movements for money
>
> Nine: This can be loneliness; someone is repeatedly fired or their job position is eliminated

If you know what the shadow aspect is of the role that you have at that job and it links back to your core values, and your vision is purpose-driven spiritual motivation, then now you have a shadow with which to work. The shadow is mirroring what you need to work through. We use these shadow aspects to help understand how to use the workplace so that we can become the CEO and the COO of our life.

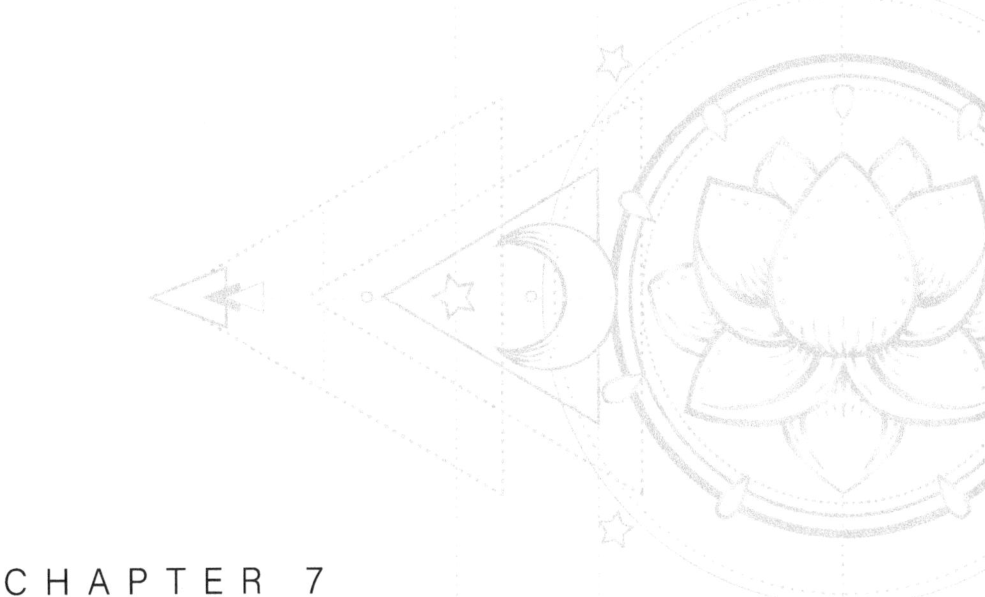

Your Work Family and How it Mirrors your Childhood Family

Work is not only material, but it's spiritual. These two consciousness levels are our dual consciousness of spirit and matter. The rational and the intuitive come together so that we can be whole.

In my book *The Seven Gates: Seven Steps Beyond Self-Awareness*, I discussed the concept of the shadow, in terms of the bad buckets (shadow aspects) inherited from our parents, and these shadow aspects show up in our colleagues as qualities we don't like as opportunities to grow ourselves and reduce conflict with others. There's a parallel between your childhood and where you work. Those creating conflict appear as shadow aspects of your parents you have not integrated yet and the same family dynamics you have at work, mimic the unresolved family dynamics of the childhood home. Your inner child appears at work hoping this time you will choose him/her and meet their needs through your interactions at work.

How you choose where you work is vibrational. Before you leave a job, do the inner work, so when you switch jobs you can have raised your consciousness and don't end up with the same job, just with different faces and location. If you haven't done the work, and you haven't raised your consciousness, you're basically just going to find another job with a different face having the same value system or the same consciousness level. You still have that work to do; the same theories, the same spiritual laws are woven through the workplace, because the workplace is dictated by the Saturn cycles.

What happened as a child and your childhood creation story is linked to the origin story of your job. Nothing creates another thing; energy cannot be created or destroyed. It is an event that arises out of a preceding event. Being at your job is not accidental. What led you to your job is directly related to those childhood years and the wounds that continue to steal your energy. As a child you could not speak up or set boundaries, at work, you revisit those same scenarios to establish your power, regain your energy and set boundaries. Those people at work that you dislike or that annoy you are your shadows, projections from your psyche and represent your metaphorical family figures so you can finally reclaim yourself.

Karma simply means action. One of the things that we do at work is work through our karma.

There are three types of karma. *Sanchitta karma* is all of your karma acquired over lifetimes. In Greek mythology, the three Fates appear at conception, and *Clotho,* one of the Fates, weaves your life at conception. She's there to design the one thread of karma you came to live out in this lifetime, known as *prarabdha karma.* It is *one* issue woven through your work, your relationships, your health issues—it's woven through everything. *Agami karma* is any karma you create in this lifetime as you live this lifecycle. Themis is the Greek goddess of justice, of karma, of foresight, of truth, of morality, of equity. Karma is dispatched to everyone equally. We may not see it equally, depending on our circumstances in life, but the law states that you get this prarabdha karma rooted in your previous deeds. So things are indeed scaled and balanced. When you think that something's out of balance, or you think that something's unjust, the law dictates otherwise. *Adrastea* is the Greek goddess who cannot be escaped. She is the goddess of revolt, retribution and sublime balance between good and evil. Work is where burning this karma plays out. The day-in and day-out process is directly linked to you becoming whole, individuated, and unified with your spiritual nature and material nature.

Lugh is one of the most prominent gods in Irish mythology. He is associated with various skills, crafts and arts. Lugh goes to the kingdom to get a job. The gentleman at the door opens the door and asks him what he is there for. He says, "I want to talk to the king, I want a job."

And the guard says, "Well, what do you do?"

He replies, "I'm a craftsman."

The guard says, "We already have someone."

Lugh tries again. "I'm a cupbearer."

The guard answers, "We already have nine of those."

Desperately, Lugh cries, "I'm a warrior!"

The guard continues to reject him. Finally, Lugh demands to speak to the king. "If I am one man who has all these skills, why wouldn't you want me?"

In a modern day and age, if you can have one employee that has all these skillsets, it doesn't mean that you're going to get rid of nine or ten other employees; you're going to utilize that employee wisely. Acquisition of skill and knowledge is important, but eventually it is wisdom we seek and value. Part of the process of work is the finetuning, and the self-growth in the work environment is to acquire more of that skill, rather, wisdom. Like Lugh, first he acquired these skills, then when he went to sell himself, the king said, "Oh, absolutely I want you on my team."

The self-worth piece is knowing that he was worth it. We've been in a society where we're not allowed to own our gifts. We're not allowed to say we're brilliant or we have strong skillsets. That is not correct. We must be the number-one marketer and self-promoter for ourselves. He was very persistent; he didn't give up. The day-to-day grind, we have to stick with it. We can't just be serial job hoppers. We should try to extract the essence of why we ended up there, because as we see, it's not chance. Knowledge of self, really knowing what you're good at and really owning that, is important. He was very good at that and yet he had practical experience. We need practical experience; education unfortunately is not enough.

There's a West African myth of two brothers. One is Mikuneri and one is Kanyanga. Mikuneri was older, and he was a little snobby. There was this old woman who came up to him in the village and said, "I can help you."

He replied, "You can't help me. You're old and blind, what do you want?"

The old lady said, "Please! Rub my eyes." But they were kind of crusty and dirty.

He was a little disgusted, so he said, "No, I'm not touching you." There was a little town down the road of small men, they weren't children. She had secrets as to how to get those small men to help Mikuneri win the kingdom. Because he didn't ask for help and he assumed that he knew everything, he failed at the task.

His younger brother, on the other hand, did help the woman. He did remove the crust from her eyes! She was then able to give him some insight.

She told him how to deal with the small men on the island, and he was able to win the prize.

Everybody at your office is an archetype. One in particular is the sherpa, or commoner, who you may deem, a "nobody"; someone you simply see as a resource. Don't discard anything or anyone, because you don't know who has the wisdom that you may not have. Always have your ears up to listen. Kanyanga used everyone as a resource; he stayed humble, which is part of the flexibility that we learn at work—the different power currency. He actually won at the task.

Childhood and Family Effects in Work

In our younger years, we do not get to work through our childhood traumas. It's during these years of work that we actually get to work through these. That's why the sixth house is the day-to-day. It's like tending the land, which is our body, our illness, our health, our happiness, our contentment, and our joy. All of this happens in the workplace, but we must bring those sorts of characters from our family life to our workspace so we can see the parallels.

Causality is a philosophical term referring to the law of cause and effect, where one event, process, state or object contributes to the production or another event. Your workplace resembles your family home and your childhood. At work, you have an origin story. Did you respond to an advertisement, did a friend tell you about it, what happened at the interview? How was the offer conceived? Your job has good buckets, and your job has bad buckets. Sit down and write that out.

What's the child script? Remember, there are two parts to the child script. What would you describe yourself as in that role in the family from years zero to seven? That could be why were you hired, or your version of why you were hired. The other part is the prophecy, which is what other people say about you as a child. What do other people say about you at work? What have you heard through the halls? What are people's keywords to describe you? How others would describe you is how you show up at work and how you will directly relate to how you fulfill the role. You want to know what's being said so you can identify what role you're trying to fulfill. Link it back to your role in your family.

What was the snow globe crack at work? Maybe it was the minute you saw your first paycheck. I mean, there was something that at that moment, the fantasy of the snow globe, of this new job, of this great location, of this great paycheck, of this great job title, was shattered.

What's the parenting style at work? There are three main parenting styles in childhood homes that carry over to the workplace. The first is the authoritative, which is the tender teacher. This is a parent that gives you rules and consequences, but they care about your opinion. They validate your feelings, they don't say, "No, that's not really what happened," or "That's not what you feel." They don't invalidate you. Research shows that these children are happier, they're more capable, they're more successful, and they're more self-disciplined. This work environment is more of a trust work environment. It's an environment where your boss will obviously give you consequences or give you reviews but allows you to speak up freely without fear.

Authoritarian style is the rigid ruler, scolding the child. They impose authority without exception. It leads to children who are obedient and proficient. The research shows these children have less happiness, social competence, and self-esteem. These are not the Lughs of the world, these are not the people that are going to show up and say, "I should get a raise because …" or "These are my competencies …" These people tend to end up in more fear-based work environments.

Then there are permissive parents who let you do most anything. They're quite lenient; they might interject if there's a severe issue. You got kicked out of school or some major drama; maybe you went to jail for shoplifting. It's usually that attention-seeking behavior. These children act out because they want to have the attention of the parents, but the parent doesn't even really discourage bad choices or bad behavior. This could be someone who has their own business, who doesn't really like to have an environment where they're not the boss. With uninvolved parents, the children raise themselves; they basically have no parental figure whatsoever.

The most expensive real estate is the real estate in your head. What thoughts about work take up space in your head? Is it the paycheck? Is it the schedule? Is that you're going to get in trouble later? These are things directly related to your childhood traumas, your unmet needs, your wounds of feeling inadequate, abandoned, not enough. There are competitive voices and collaborative voices that live in your head. The competitive voices are those that show up to tell you you're not enough. I call mine the perfect older sister.

Perfectionism at work is linked to your parents; they show up with the parenting style of the institution, your leader, your boss, your direct supervisor or your manager. That parenting style shows up because it is there for you to work through, for you to grow in wisdom as an adult. Is your head psychologically safe or is it dangerous? Is it safe to be in those thoughts? Are you processing those thoughts? This can contribute to your mental health, your spiritual well-being, or it can be really damaging, self-inflicting, damaging thoughts.

Mokitas is a term from Papua New Guinea that speaks to the elephant in the room that many people won't address at work because they have an authoritarian work environment. In leadership or in the workplace, there are fear-based cultures. In the workplace, these are competitive voices in the head. Where there's a lot of tension, perhaps there's a lot of authority, there's a lot of rules, rigidity. Everything is very punitive. So a fear-based culture is all happening in your head and manifesting in your workplace. These environments specialize in assigning work, measuring results, punishing infractions, and maintaining order. There is some gatekeeper at the door, they're watching the clock, you've got to punch in, you've got to meet your minutes. There really isn't much emphasis even on quality, perhaps. It might be more of a quantity place; it's all about the metrics. Not even in using the metrics to grow, it's just about checking lists and so forth. People that live in this sort of fear-based culture or have this going on in their head are psychologically dangerous. They have a constant fear of losing their job, they're afraid to tell the truth, they question all the time. That's one of the penetrating thoughts, "*Will I have a job?*" They live with fear and suspicion about who's saying what, who's doing what, are there spies, things like that. There's resentment that develops as a result.

This is directly linked to a lack of safety and security needs from childhood. This is directly linked to authoritarian parents, fear and punishment parenting. Obedience and compliance, that's not about validating feelings. If you're in a fear-based culture you're there to work through these voices in your head, these archetypes from childhood.

Daniel Pink, author of *Drive: The Surprising Truth About What Motivates Us,* discusses the seven deadly flaws directly related to a work experience. This can extinguish motivation when we don't feel safe in a workplace. A fear-based culture diminishes performance, it crushes creativity, it crowds out good behavior, because there's so much focus on the punitive. The bad encourages shortcuts, cheating, and unethical behavior. People are seeing how to break the rules. If we link this to childhood, people that have such oppressive, fear-based childhood or authoritarian parents are always looking to see how to sneak out. How can they can get away with something? It becomes a shadow aspect to your psyche, because you need to release the oppressor. You need freedom from these oppressing thoughts in this oppressing parenting style. This is no different at work. He says that it can become addictive, what I call psychological homeostasis, creating the psychological orgasm, trying to get your unmet needs met, proving repeatedly that you're not enough, or you're abandoned. This is the exact environment that you would want to get out of. It actually feeds your unmet needs, feeds the childhood trauma, feeds that vicious cycle of child thinking and child behavior. This is actually quite addictive, he says, and it fosters short-term thinking. You're not ever thinking long-term goals, *wisdom*. Five, ten-year plans are not on your radar; you're just in the wounding moment from childhood. The subconscious gets stuck there. It's like emotional hunger. You're just trying to get your needs met and so it's a vicious cycle that perpetuates. Pink calls this psychological danger, which starts with fear of admitting mistakes, blaming others. You don't share different viewpoints, so it becomes a homogenous culture, because no one wants to share an opinion or an idea. It becomes what's known as the *common knowledge effect*; it's the status quo in the office, and nothing is ever challenged or tried to do differently.

The collaborative voices are those aspects in your head that get along. This type of work environment is rooted in psychological safety and is a trust-based culture. The Harvard professor Amy Edmondson coined the term *psychological safety* for the workplace. You're not humiliated or punished if you come up with an idea, if you talk about a concern, or if you address mistakes, yours or your colleagues or even leaders. This leads to more innovation, increased productivity, an authentic environment of candor, and is directly linked to authoritative parenting. Your needs are maybe not fully met, since no child's needs are completely met, but there might be a validation factor here, or at least having your emotions be acknowledged. People in this sort of work environment are comfortable admitting their mistakes. They openly will say, "Oh, I'm sorry I made a mistake," or "Let me try to fix that." They learn from their failures, everyone openly shares their ideas, and no one's ridiculed or criticized. It creates a more innovative workplace and better decision making, because everyone's involved in the decision-making process.

Pink says there are three levels of motivation linked to work environments. The trust- or fear-based cultures' motivation is basic survival, linked to safety and security needs. You are in fear all the time when you're in a fight-or-flight mode, in an adrenaline rush, in a constant struggle to not get fired; just surviving. There are childhood homes that resemble that same thing.

Motivation 2.0 is when you seek reward and avoid punishment. This is also very childish, because "good boy morality" is simply so it appears that you're doing good. This creates karma. This is part of that agami karma that we don't want to keep creating. We will create additional karma if we show up just acting like a good girl or good boy. A friend once shared a story that someone at their job painted the wall without any permission. The person who oversaw the project was like, "I now have to undo what you've done." It appeared as if the intention was altruistically motivated, although we know it's not. It's back to this: the reward and the punishment. So this person without knowing it, subconsciously, was either wanting to seek a reward or a punishment to repeat that sort of childhood pattern.

Pink says that Motivation 3.0 is linked much more to trust-based cultures. Authoritative parenting is to seek autonomy, mastery, and purpose. This is the Lugh. Where you can show up, you can be autonomous. Maybe you're in control of your own schedule. Self-mastery is skill and knowledge, but also, self-mastery is using the workplace to learn about mistakes. As mentioned, mokitas is a Papua New Guinea term, and it means "everybody knows, but no one talks about." We've all been there: it's the elephant in the room, there's one in every family. It's the "hush-hush" whispered, no one says it but it energetically just looms. More fear-based cultures have this idea, and so some companies have gone a step further to say, what is your mokita? What is it that internally you carry?

This is a project or an assignment you can give your employees or your clients. What is the personal mokita? What's going on in the workplace? Make it anonymous and start the process to begin airing the dirty laundry and get clarity in the workplace. Research shows the fewer mokitas, the healthier the business, and this is directly linked to wearing fewer masks at work. The fewer masks you wear, the fewer mokitas, the healthier you are.

In 2012, Google launched an initiative called *Project Aristotle*. They wanted to know what made a healthy workplace using the term psychological safety. They wanted to know what qualities created a psychologically safe workplace. They learned that no one wants to put on a "work face." You don't have to go to work and put on a face like nothing's wrong, that everything's okay. Google also learned that no one wants to leave a part of their personality and inner life at home. They obviously understood that work is the sacred space, where you spend time with people the most. All archetypes are there, all family members are there, all aspects of your psyche are there. Why would you want to leave your inner life at home when one of the key components of work is to sort through stuff and cultivate your inner life? Lastly, they found that ideally, you're able to talk about what is messy or sad. Have hard conversations, even about your own colleagues. Tell your colleague that they are lazy or that they didn't do a good job. It's about being comfortable in the discomfort.

I once asked a client, would you rather be uncomfortably comfortable or comfortably numb? We're so used to just being numb and robotic. Illness is only one of these ways that we have permission to be sad and grieving, or not okay. We can actually reduce that if we create environments that are safe for people to have messy, hard conversations, and they learn something called C = R = C, which means conversation is the relationship, is the culture. The conversations that you're having are building the relationships in the workforce and that builds the culture. What they want to do is build a psychologically safe culture.

Nobody comes from that at home. We do not have safety and security needs met in childhood, unfortunately; this is the adult archetype. This is the Saturn archetype, this is the exact space where we're supposed to cultivate these sort of adulting and spiritual adulting demands. It really is the equation C = R = C.

I grew up in a cult and learned that cults are rooted in coercion; however, during an existential crisis at thirty-three, I screamed and yelled to the Universe and asked for an answer. A book from the Kabbalah tradition, called *The Zohar*, fell off the shelf and opened to a quote that gave me an understanding I hadn't previously had, and it read "There is no coercion in spirituality."

Fortunately, not everyone grows up in a cult, but everyone grows up in a coercive family environment where your needs are not met. You may need to get good grades so your parents look good, and perhaps you need to look a certain way to maintain the family image—this is coercion. The definition of a cult is a devotion directed towards a particular figure or object, in this case, your parents. We really do have a cult in our head, and the subconscious programming dictating 99 percent of our lives is the cultish programming from your parents, which started at conception. Common sayings that may have framed your subconscious were "children should be seen and not heard," "girls are made of sugar and spice and everything nice," "never trust your tongue when your heart is bitter" and a bunch of other adages spewed in your childhood home by adults—that's coercion. There is coercion in families, and there are parent-child coercive cycles, some intentional, most not, but it is to shape the child's behavior to the parent's disciplinary style so the child backs down during negative parent-child interactions.

Gerald Patterson from the University of Oregon and Oregon Social Learning Center studied the worsening behavior in children and loss of control in parents, which follows a sequence he termed The *Parent-Child Coercive Cycle.* These same cycles and however you experienced them in childhood, mild or harsh, show up in your work environment to work through. Whatever your particular story was, a link to coerciveness will show up in your work environment. In the context of spiritual abuse, it is defined as coercion or control of one individual by another. In cults and religious organizations, the cult leader, guru or God is the figurehead. Well, it's no different in a parental unit, where the parents are the figureheads and it's no different in a work unit, where the supervisors may be the figurehead. It's coercive and abusive. Again, according to the Law of Correspondence, it is happening without and externally, because it is happening in your head. It is your program of low self-worth or insecurity that creates the coercive environment or authority figurehead you're responding to negatively, in your head. Everyone has had some version of this; even permissive parents demonstrate coercion. It could be the absence of parenting and forced early adulthood that is the coercion.

We are all playing this out, in different degrees, in our home life as children, in our heads, and therefore in our work environments. Manipulation, gaslighting, violence, whether workplace violence, domestic violence or family violence, even the silent treatment or going without supper, is emotional abuse and manipulation; it exists in every household. It does not have to be physical. A common one I hear with clients is, "I'm so disappointed in you." This is emotional coercion and a power play. If your needs are not met, which I established earlier, there is a link to coercion. Having to be a certain something will lead to perfectionism, or at least some criticism if you don't live up to the expectation, in order to get a conditional, Costco-version of love (a metaphor for bulk conditional love we all receive in some fashion or another) that your parents were offering you. This is coercive in nature.

On a scale of one to ten, somewhere in your psyche that shattered snow globe of your childhood family cult must show up in your workplace. You might get shunned at work by a certain group of people. There might be guilt trips if you don't go to the meetings or the softball club after work. This is the polar opposite to freedom. Coercion is the polar opposite to freedom; compliance is the goal. Any coercive mechanism is to get you to comply in an authoritarian coercive fashion. This is the key to lacking individuation, to a herd mentality, to the low-level mass consciousness.

Individuation is the purpose of answering the call, as Joseph Campbell called it in the *Hero's Journey*. In my twelve truths model, it is linked to the

Truth of Personality, Ego & Soul and is linked to the solar archetype, which is what I like to call having an STD: say, think and do as a unified consciousness. However, rather than responding to the cult or coercive techniques in your psyche, you honor your truth. That sort of low-level consciousness of the manager, of the mass thinking, it's the exact opposite of saying, thinking, and doing, of becoming a no sayer.

We're all experiencing this somewhere in our life. Somewhere there's a coercion. There's something that stems from childhood that you will see in your workplace relationships. This directly leads to perfectionism, one of the competitive voices in our heads.

In the movie *Mother's Day* the main character was a widow left to raise two daughters. The older girl starting sneaking out and dating, and dad freaked out. At one point the perfect older sister who had been the perfect soccer star and had the straight A's yelled at the dad, "I cook for you, I clean for you, I take care of my sister. I need a life, you know." This perfectionism, or this voice of doing everything perfectly, is directly linked to competitiveness. It's directly linked to being compared.

Somewhere you were compared, somewhere there was a competition, and you didn't measure up, or you measured up so well that you collapsed. This is directly linked to anxiety rates in mental health, transcendental narcissism, the sick role and illness. Many years ago, I was Dean of Academics at a nursing school, and I learned that nurses are typically perfectionists and overachievers. If you think about it, the doctor sends the orders, and the nurses must make sure that they're doing it right. They have to check the prescription and that they're not making medication errors. There's a lot of pressure in that job, not to mention the compassion, the warmth and caring that you must give. It's a very high-stress job. The nursing director on campus was a perfectionist, and I would tell her repeatedly: seek excellence, not perfection. Perfection doesn't exist, it automatically sets you up for failure. It's zero to a hundred, it's a total child script. It's a shadow aspect to the Neptune archetype of codependence, innocence and inferiority.

I will sometimes find myself identifying in a personal TED talk that I'm judging perfection because that was one of the big things from my childhood in the coercive cult environment. If you use that and you identify perfection, you know that there's competitiveness, you know that there's comparison, and it's a no-win situation. Shift the mindset to strive for excellence, not perfection. It's directly linked to low self-worth, abandonment issues, and criticism. Anxiety is linked to perfectionism. People that are perfectionists are obsessive and inefficient at work. They have a multitude of serious mental health issues that affect attendance, performance and morale. You'll often see a perfectionist procrastinate because she's afraid of failing even before she starts. Alternatively she may position herself as a martyr, the only one who cares, thinks, or worries enough about getting things right. Yet it's a vicious cycle: nothing gets done, or they are out sick because they are so afraid to even start the project for fear of failure.

Failure, perfection, and excellence—these things are very important to identify in yourself. How they're triggered in a work environment is directly linked to fear of individuation. *When They Zig, You Zag* is a book by Siimon Reynolds. It means you're going your own way, you're finding your own divine expression within the rules. He says, don't follow the crowds. People that are perfectionists don't want to zig when others zag. They're afraid of criticism, judgment, standing out, being different and being ridiculed. It's directly linked to not wanting to individuate and remain a child psychologically. The famous mythologist Joseph Campbell in his book *A Hero with a Thousand Faces* gave the metaphor of the life path the name the Hero's Journey, indicating that when we are called to individuate and carve our own path, we should heed the call. His famous slogan was "follow your bliss." Follow your bliss does not mean do whatever you wish without regard for others; it simply means follow your calling, your thread of divinity in this lifetime.

Individuation is a Jungian term that allows the individual to access the totality of his humanity, and subsequently fosters self-regard and the development of social interests, with a focus on the Self, not exclusively the ego. The buddha used a term called bodhisattva, which is someone who's gradually becoming the buddha. This spiritual, wise person understands that everything is sacred space and uses all environments to get self-realized. They're both about becoming whole.

Gurdjieff believed that man has no individuality. He has no single, big "I," but rather many separate small "I's" and calls himself whole. Many years ago, I worked at the National Institutes of Health, and I was a nutritionist for a study. A colleague was hired named Doris, and my boss called me into the office one day and said "Doris does this, Doris does that."

I looked at her and I said, "Do you want two Dorises or do you want a Doris and a Frances?"

She looked at me and said, "Oh no, I want a Doris and a Frances."

And I said, "Okay we have the same job, but we're going to do it differently."

You must individuate within the job description. You have to bring your way, your divinity through your humanity. I went to an all-girls Catholic school, and we wore uniforms. I wanted to stand out, so I started wearing funky shoes and cool socks. I was trying to individuate. Jung would call this individualism, where the person identifies with the ego, resulting in a type of narcissism, where everything revolves around the needs and rights of the ego. Joseph Campbell has often been misrepresented with "follow your bliss" to mean individualism, not individuation. It's healthy to find your personality or your spark within the rules. Break the rules, within the rules. We're all human, let's not get sick or try to be perfect. Let's allow our own divine spark. It's about finding your bodhisattva, your individuation process, your realization, your wholeness within the rules, within the confines of being human.

Rob Preece wrote *The Wisdom of Imperfection*. Perfect doesn't exist; it's our imperfections that make us perfect. Like Campbell's *The Hero's Journey* or my *Twelve Truths to a Spiritual Adult*, it's a path. A path is person-centered, it's spirit-focused, it involves insights to Self. When you're at work, you can have both a process-centered divinity and a material focus. There are procedures, policies, doctrine and a mission to the organization. Fine, follow that process. That's part of your material growth. It gets you your paycheck or your raise at the end of the year. It's material, it's clear and concise. You need that. However, within the work environment, find a path. Something that's personal, individuated, and person-centered. Something that's about using the Principle of Correspondence, showing up with spirit consciousness so that you can grow, integrate and individuate, while meeting your material needs. The workplace should be both a path and a process.

Do you want both to be at work? Do you just want to follow a process? Do you just want to be told what to do? Go in, do your eight hours, clock out, and that's it. The parenting style at work is very much linked to your parenting style from childhood. We all do have a perfect older sister voice somewhere in the competitive matrix of our head. The *Eisenhower Decision Matrix* is used for people in leadership to designate what they're going to do in terms of their workload. People get caught up in the minutia and the small details and miss the bigger picture. One of your roles as a leader is to help people categorize, if you will, their work and the importance of their work. Eisenhower stated that there's urgent and important work, that's obviously a priority; urgent, but not important; not urgent, but important; not urgent and not important.

Funny enough, oftentimes a perfectionist will spend time on nonurgent and unimportant work because they know how to do it. It's process-oriented work, it's easy, there are steps, there's a checklist, it's routine, it's written. So other areas are left abandoned. They don't follow through on the bigger, more urgent, more important work in their work lives, personal lives or spiritual lives, all out of fear.

The Eisenhower Decision Matrix

The Eisenhower Decision Matrix also known as the Urgent-Important Matrix is used for time management and helps you prioritize your tasks based on urgency and importance.

There are certain things that you have to do first, there are things that you do later, and there are things that you delegate. When you fail to delegate, it's greedy (in a Neptunian way). Not delegating is part of a low self-worth issue, because you think you have ultimate control, and we have control of nothing. There are certain things that you completely eliminate, that you choose that there's no time in your day, in your schedule, to do. You might suffer a consequence, but you must make those choices. You have to do this same thing in your life.

Some of the research says that if you do tend to have this perfectionism, break out of that by finding something distracting. Something menial to break the pattern of the constant thinking around perfectionism. Learning to delegate is important. Does the extra time impact your life or your job for the better? It is known that perfectionists will spend so much time on something making it "perfect" that does not add anything to the presentation, anything to the outcome of the goal, the mission, and the vision of the company or to the sales pitch. Nothing! There is no real accountability around how that extra time impacts and makes something more successful, more money or whatever the metric is.

There is a diminishing return. You can work so much toward perfection that you come right back and it has no payoff whatsoever. This is this vicious cycle of this perfect older sister voice linked to childhood and family trends.

You do need to have some personal standards. Your values and a checklist guide you. When is a project, a PowerPoint or an assignment just right? So you don't waste valuable time and resources on perfection that doesn't exist. *Psychological distance* is the idea of separating yourself from a phenomenon, for instance, recapping at the end of the day, or at the end of the week. Track your progress. Did I avoid something for fear of making mistakes? I often give this as homework to clients as a self-reflective tool to see where they let perfectionism seep into their life. Since subconsciously we are stuck in a child script, our unmet needs show up at work.

Unmet Needs at Work

Five of the most common ways that unmet needs show up at work include:

1. You're jealous, insecure and you dissociate.
2. You become a recluse. You want nothing to do with people or situations. You may not even respond to some communications.
3. You're very clingy, you have fear of abandonment. You may be in the boss's office all the time seeking approval, or you're always trying to get lunch dates with colleagues.
4. You morph into what everyone wants you to be so you don't have individuation. You don't necessarily have an identity; you'll be anything for everybody.
5. You put people on pedestals.

When you are between zero and seven years old, there are several moments, but there tends to be one that sticks out, where you were blamed, shamed or guilted, and you realized you were not accepted exactly as you are: this is what I call your snow globe shattering event. Your inner child was created at this moment, along with your ego and personality and what your inner child heard was, *"That is not acceptable in this family, you're not enough as you are, you're worthless!"* You can identify whether you consciously or subconsciously remember the story, but your inner child remembers it, and every day, every moment that is a conflict, the wound reopens, and your perfect older sister voice reminds you how you're not enough. At that moment, you learned, *"I'm not enough, I will be abandoned if I don't save face."*

Since you weren't enough as you are, you created what Jung calls a *persona*, an ego or personality to show up in the world and save face, all the while covering up your true Self. these are the masks we wear, in hopes of getting unconditional love and our needs met. It never happens. It is an inside job. The individuation process reveals your true self, both flawed human and divine, and the process teaches you that you are enough just as you are; thereby, you begin meeting your own needs and loving yourself unconditionally. The recurring impure thought, *"I need to be more"* is linked to perfectionism. Perfectionism is one of the results of the child wound, it is a child script, a zero-to-one-hundred pendulum swing. By totally dissociating, they try to avoid ever being caught in the crossfire again. The mystical enneagram is a tool that can also be used to track the age the subconscious felt it got stuck or abandoned. If you can recall the first moment of shame or rejection from ages 1-9 you can identify the shadow aspect you are working through in the work environment. Your inner child is with you wherever you go, including work. If your work environment represents your childhood family and trauma, the inner child shows up in these situations to attempt healing and growth. Shadow numbers relate to your childhood wound and what your inner child needs to integrate to feel safe and grow. Recall the age of the shame and find the shadow aspect on the chart.

1. Perfectionist	Intolerant
2. Obsessed	Fixated
3. Ruthless	Deception
4. Self-loathing	Low self-esteem
5. Withdrawn, disconnected	Psychotic
6. Confusion, contradictory	Chaotic
7. Excess, addiction	Suicide
8. Attention, hard-heart	Violent & destructive
9. Numb	Denial

Everyone's inner child got "stuck" an age between zero and nine due to a subconscious trauma. The age you were stuck is linked to a shadow aspect listed above. Your work number is linked to what you are attempting to heal in your psyche and with your inner child.

Where's the individuation? Where is the bodhisattva? Where is this wholeness? This integrative capacity is linked to your work number. There's a lesson in each number, something for the inner child to integrate to achieve wholeness and individuation. Below are keywords linked to the enneagram number that can help you to identify what to integrate at work.

One: Serenity
Two: Humility
Three: Authenticity & Truthfulness
Four: Balance & Equanimity
Five: Detachment
Six: Courage
Seven: Sobriety
Eight: Innocence; Purity of Thought
Nine: Action

Depending on your role in that particular job, you can learn through these lessons what you're there to learn as a spiritual path, versus the process which would be more materially related.

Forgiveness

There's a lot of literature on forgiveness, and honestly, I am all about forgiveness of self. I don't think we forgive others or another forgives us. Forgiveness is about self. If you don't forgive yourself, there's no forgiveness. As I do with most things, I bring it back to the Self. It's all about ourselves. At what level of spiritual consciousness did I create the problem? Why did I create this? Why did I allow this to enter my sphere of consciousness? What do I have to learn from it?

There is a lot of research on forgiveness in the workplace. In 2012, this company called Courageous Leadership worked with Google to build what they call a courageous culture, and one of the things they worked on was forgiveness. They said that that's directly linked to ongoing work relationships.

I bought a book many years ago that was on learning how to forgive. It should have been one line: Forgiveness is all about Self. If you don't forgive yourself for not being perfect, for being simply human, for being ordinary, for being chaotic, for having impure thoughts, then the child script and our lower nature keeps the real estate in our head, spending valuable energy trying to seek our unmet needs. The forgiveness of self, leads to wholeness. In spirituality, there is no other, when we integrate the aspects of ourselves that others are mirroring, the forgiveness happens internally. Where it needs to happen. Simply recognizing that the person, let's say in our workplace, that entered our consciousness, is there to mirror us, we can forgive ourselves, because we understand that we are divine despite our humanity.

Courageous Leadership found where employees shared times when they failed to act on their values at work. I think this was key. If you can identify that you self-betrayed and that you violated your nonnegotiables at work, you can begin healing. You must have a very clear value system. The Google employees admitted that they didn't understand something; that's courageous and brave. They spoke up when they thought they had a better idea than a colleague or even their boss. Imagine telling your boss, "Oh, your idea is not that great. I have a better one." This was designed to remind everyone how easy it is to act outside of our values. This is important. Values, values, values! Our entire life is simply finding our value system in measurable terms. We can't forgive ourselves, much less anybody else, because we don't even know what we're trying to forgive ourselves for or what in ourselves we're self-betraying.

Parenting style is directly linked to attachment style. Coercion, competition, comparing: this is all linked to the childhood subconscious wound created between zero and seven years old. The ability to self-forgive is linked to forgiving yourself from that moment when the inner child was created at that shattering snow globe moment in childhood, and healing that wound in turn will create a healthier environment at work. Then, possibly, you know how to forgive another.

Everett Worthington created the R.E.A.C.H. model acronym for forgiveness that's used in the workplace. R is recall the hurt; E is empathize with your partner, A is an altruistic gift, C is commit and H is hold onto forgiveness. However, I must reiterate and add a B for back again. Again, bring it back to Self, this is part of the bodhisattva. This is part of the wholeness, this is part of the individuation.

Recall the hurt and how you self-betrayed. Did you betray a value system you didn't have or admit a need that you went and coercively sought out? Empathize with your inner child who has been trying to get love and her needs met externally. Be altruistic to yourself and your inner child by having a playdate with yourself, reading him or her a story, or finally listening to what they need. Below is a chart of enneagram numbers and things you can gift your inner child to recognize him or her during the forgiveness process. Write a letter acknowledging you'll commit to inner work, a commitment to self that you're going to own, and then hold on to that and forgive yourself despite future mistakes you'll inevitably make. Forgive the perfect older sister voice when she shows up. Don't beat yourself up, recant that you're not enough, criticize yourself and fall into that vicious cycle of the psychological orgasm.

One	Wants attention. Take her out for a solo date.
Two	Wants a play date with friends.
Three	Wants to be read to. Get a children's book, a favorite from childhood maybe, and read it to him/her.
Four	Wants structure and rules. Give her a strict bedtime or a strict routine in one small thing in life. Nothing too strict.
Five	Wants to have fun and get dirty. Get playdoh and get messy. Plant something. Fingerpaint.
Six	Wants some work. Wants to build something and see her work displayed on the fridge or on the mantle. For example, Build-A-Bear, a popsicle project a Lego project.
Seven	Wants quiet and solitude. Take a bubble bath or go for a walk, alone.
Eight	Wants to spend money. Buy her/him something frivolous, just because.
Nine	Wants to end something. Throw away some old clothes or old books or burn old journals. Do not donate it. It needs to clearly end by throwing it away, not passing it down to others.

Your inner child is asking for attention. What number at you at in your current work role based on the enneagram? Find the number above which indicates the specific need your inner child has and how to satisfy that need for him/her.

Leadership Wheel

I created these twelve values around my definition of leadership. I have them very clearly defined in measurable, definable terms, and I identify the zero-to-one hundred swings so I can catch myself returning to a child script and a perfect older sister voice. You can make your own criteria, but they seem to encompass a lot of key values that leaders possess or wish to possess.

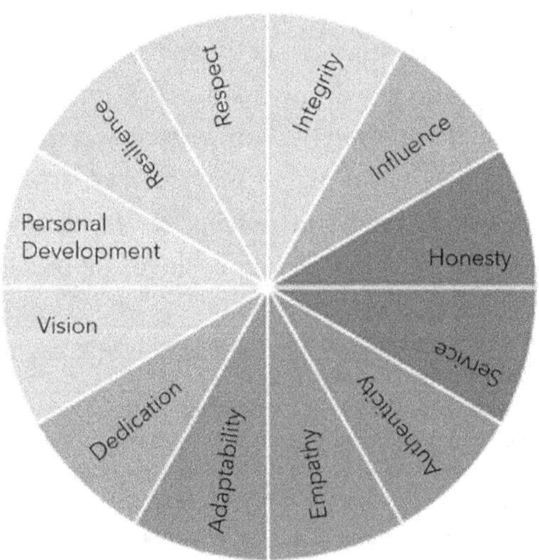

Vision. How do you see yourself? What's your role in the organization? What are your expectations around this job?

Dedication: Again, your values. What do you buy into? What incongruences are there between your values and the organization's values? Do they overlap? Are they self-serving? Are they self-betraying? Do they violate your nonnegotiables? Do you value yourself? If you value yourself, then how are you going to show up with your time, your money, and your resources? Are you going to ask for the appropriate salary, or will you cower when that conversation comes up? Are you going to ask for raises, are you going to leave when it's time to leave? Unless, of course, there's some big event that you need to prepare for. Are you going to honor your values?

Adaptability: This has to be with thoughts, and you're going to use the workplace to allow others to mirror to you your impure thoughts and the way you think about yourself.

Empathy: Are your needs met through this job? You must meet your needs; that's your responsibility. Is the job helping you to see your thoughts and meet your own needs?

Authenticity: Are you of value to your employer? Do you show up as yourself, balanced, or are you one of those people that morphs with whatever they need? Do you put people on a pedestal? Do you view yourself as authentic and show up balanced in life?

Service: Are you a container for the mission and the vision of the organization? Again, you've got to check the mission and the vision. Does this align with your values? Do you like the mission and the vision?

Honesty: Do you contribute honestly? Do you promote the values of the organization or are you embarrassed? Do you lie, or cower at the idea of anyone knowing that you worked there?

Influence: Are you making a difference? Do you have a position of influence? Not necessarily in the organization, but do you feel that you're an influential member of the team? Do you model the values of the organization in your personal life? Would the same person in your personal and your professional life have the same value system?

Integrity: Again, are your personal values and the organization in alignment? Because that would be truth.

Respect: Do you spread the mission? You have to believe in something to spread it.

Resilience: Do you knock down negativity with clear communication? This does not mean put on a smile, everything's great, positive vibes only. That is not what I'm about at all. It's, do we clear the air, do we talk about the mokitas, the elephant in the room, through clear communication?

Personal Development: Are you in union with the organization? Does this spiritually serve you? Does it serve the community? I told you that astrologically, we bring ourselves in individually in our work life. Over here in this personal sector, we work through spirituality with our material and spiritual parts. Then we go out into the community and become social beings, influential people withs vocations who give back to society. If the employer is not serving you, a whole person, then how are you going to give back to the community? You're still sort of down here, getting basic needs met because you're in a fear-based culture.

Five C's of Diamond Leadership

When you go diamond shopping, there are the four C's: *Cut, Color, Clarity and Carat*. I add *Consciousness*, since that's what mental and spiritual health is all about.

Cut. Cut is the most important influencer on the sparkle of the diamond. What do you want to look like after the process of this job, of taking this job? When you take on the job, what is it that you want to look like afterwards? What are you going to purify? What are you going to carve away? Michelangelo said that making the David was super easy: he just chipped away at the excess, the David was already in the slab of marble. What are you going to be chipping away at during this job? What's that going to make you look like after the process? This is very much linked to your divine will and your purpose. You must know your values to get there. This will also identify your low-level consciousness. Why are you working in a place? What is it that you're going to work through? Let's say it's a fear culture. Maybe you're working on coercion, or you're working on comparison. After this job ends, in a week, two weeks, three years or thirty years, it doesn't matter, how will you improve as a result of this job?

Color. Next is color. The less color, when it comes to diamonds, the better. This is linked to the spiritual striptease. The less veils you wear, the better. What Google established was that you don't have a mask that you wear at work and one for at home; instead, show up whole and individuated. Bring the good, the bad and the ugly to work. Less personality and more soul. I told you that personality is like the mask that we wear to blend in, where soul is the individuation process where you show up, warts and all. This is going to require constant TED talks. What are you thinking? What are your emotions? What are your desires? According to this, what are you judging? So that you can get clearer, and clearer, in your color. How can the job help you be more authentic, perhaps? What can you learn from those archetypes that you dislike or the elements you dislike?

Clarity. Next is clarity. In diamond speak, clarity is regarding tiny imperfections, and they're not that important to the price or the quality at the end of the day. It's really about understanding, appreciating and forgiving your imperfections. Find that divinity through the humanity. How is it that you can do it? What zig when others are zagging can you bring to the job, to the role into the organization? How do those quirks and differences benefit the organization? How can you be a Frances and not a Doris, so that everybody can get both?

Carat. Carat is directly linked to the weight of the diamond. You have weight, which is linked to self-worth and how you manage your time, money, resources and your presence at work.

Consciousness. The last C, which is personally the most important for me, is consciousness. Raising consciousness is all that this is about. Are you using the job to grow spiritually? Are you looking at the parallels from your snow globe from your unmet needs, from the parenting style, from coercion, from comparison, from your wound, from childhood? Seeing how this job can really help you work through those things that you couldn't do with your parents as a child? What archetypes are you incorporating? When you have that list of archetypes, in any way that you look at them, if you start adding those archetypes in or integrating them, you're growing spiritually and raising consciousness. Because after awareness comes integration; then you could do it differently.

Carl Jung wrote a book called *Answer to Job*. Job in the Bible was a man who endured a lot of pain and suffering. Carl Jung wrote an answer to Job in response to that Bible story. He said, "Whoever knows God, has an effect on him." It seems narcissistic; maybe it seems a little like hubris, and it's prideful to think that you matter in any capacity, that God would care, but Jung said that you do.

The reality is that our human consciousness affects creation. We are cruel creators in this Universe. It goes back to that cause and effect. We create the world we live in; it's all happening in our heads. So everything we're creating at the level of poverty, social injustice, or workplace fear, we're participating in that. We do matter to the Universe at a consciousness level. We impact absolutely everything and everyone. What we are matters, monumentally. If we go to work. If we continue the process of our child script. If we're just process rather than path-oriented, and we separate from the divine. From our divine self, from our spiritual nature. From using work as a sacred space, using work as dharma. Using work to define our values, our mission, our vision for our personal leadership and our personal lives. Then we separate from the role that we actually came to play at a larger scale.

Individuation helps to enrich the storehouse consciousness. *Storehouse consciousness* is a term that Buddhists use for why people return so often to the same emotional states and viewpoints, an unconscious level of experience where your habits are maintained and where they transform. Jung calls it the collective unconscious, the part of the mind containing memories and impulses of which the individual is not aware. We are all working symbolically, and symbol, myth, metaphor, the language of the Universe, is stored in the subconscious. It's connected to everything else; that's why when we see a color or symbol, it's all stored in Jung's collective unconscious or in Buddha's storehouse consciousness. When we individuate, we give another version to that story, to that symbol, to the way that it can be done humanly and divinely.

Jung visited with the Navajo people, and they shared a story where the tribal members participated in helping their sun god cross the sky each day. Basically what that meant was, you are indispensable for the completion of creation. You are needed in your family, you're needed in your workplace. You're needed in the world. Your individuation process adds to this and what this all becomes. Whether you're speaking at the family level, at the individual level, at the work level, or at the universal level, it's only through raising your consciousness via individuation. Becoming that bodhisattva healing, that perfectionism you know. Becoming excellent rather than trying to be perfect and creating trust and self-forgiveness. You can weave your story, your individuated high consciousness story into the fabric of the world.

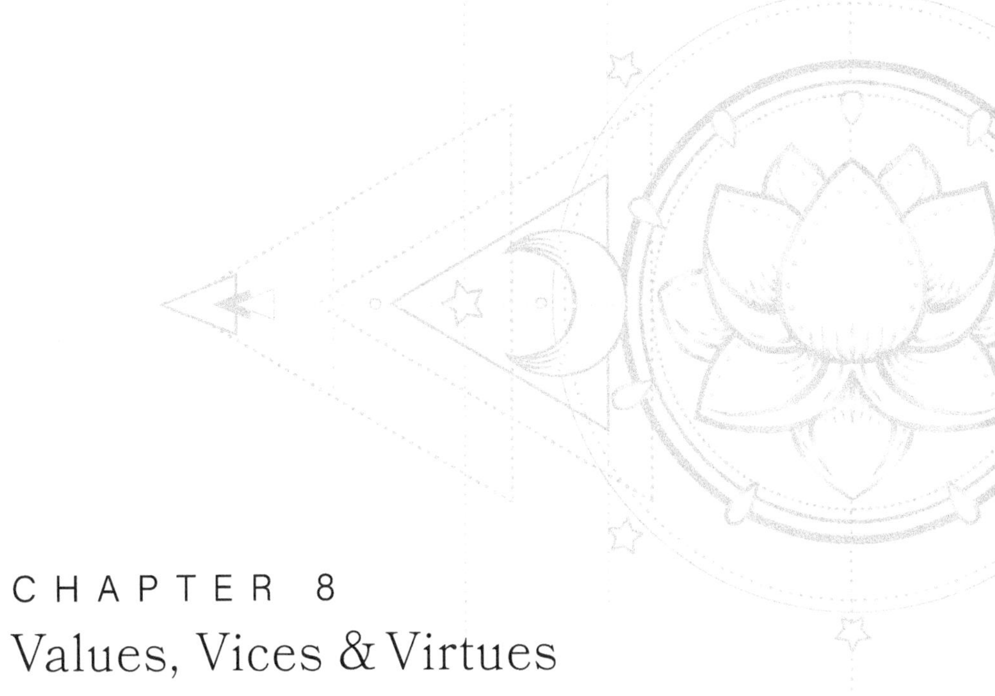

Values, Vices & Virtues

Health, workplace wellness, and illness are linked to your value systems. Work is sacred space, teaching us to be an everyday man, day-in and day-out at work as the commoner. Yet, being divine as we find our originality and individuate all the while, we identify that everything is a reflection of self and created for us to learn, bend and become supple. Why do we spend so much time at work? What is the function of work from a soul perspective? It's to integrate all the different archetypes, the aspects of self, and to bend, learn and achieve wisdom and skill.

Everything is energy. How we spend our energy in the earthly world is linked to time, money, and resources, and linked to us getting sick or if we stay healthy. This is linked to our value system; where we spend our time, energy, and resources is directly linked to our values. Look at your calendar, or where they spend their time, their energy, and their resources. Work is the intersection of your own personal values and corporate values. *Nerio* was the Roman goddess of war, strength and the personification of valor. Virtus was the Roman god of bravery, living out our value system often feels like an act of war which requires strength and bravery.

If you show up for yourself with a clear value system, what are you choosing to lose when the time comes to commit to that value system? It seems a little ironic that we are afraid to be ourselves, show up for ourselves, have a value system, have valor and be healthy. Yet, it's something we have not been given permission to do. No one has received a template where they have permission to individuate; that's why it feels like war in the mind. It takes bravery, courage, and a solid value system to achieve. Gluttonous thinking is all or none (0-100) thinking. Wanting to believe a thought is true, 100% of the time, is gluttonous thinking. This is taught verbally or non-verbally in childhood. In *The Seven Gates: Seven Steps Beyond Self-Awareness* I offer a chart of blanket value statements that many of us have heard in childhood. (i.e., work before play, children should be seen not heard, there's no free lunch) and without a strong value system to limit the gluttonous thought, we subconsciously infuse these statements into our thoughts and behaviors and unknowingly live them in a 0-100 fashion. Once you limit a thought, what I call "Yes, and thinking" you can believe the statement; however, set conditions and limits on when it is true. This requires a strong value system and is how the sage archetype helps to limit the innocent archetype and child thinking becomes self-mastery. *Asclepius*, considered the god of medicine, was given the name because it means to "cut open." Be curious about your psyche. Cut yourself open. Dissect yourself. What are you made of? What are your values? What are your thoughts? Those deep dark shadow aspects? Because when we cut ourselves open, we can see what our thoughts, emotions and desires (TED) are that we are buying into without even questioning what it is doing to our lives. This is ultimately the first step towards self-mastery and true behavior change. In the Egyptian mythology, the *Hall of Maat* is where you entered when you died. The goddess of justice, *Anubis*, would take your heart put it on a scale next to *Maat's* feather and if your heart was lighter than a feather you would go to the next life. If your heart was heavier than *Maat's* feather, then you would go to the underworld. Think of the importance of having the lightness of heart, virtue and bravery. Living by your value systems. This is the crux of our mental health, our physical health and our spiritual health. What does your heart want to be weighed against? What sort of template? The word *valere* means to be in good health in Latin. The word value or values comes from this valere, creator of value, establisher of vital norms. We are given our value system at the moment of conception, and most of us are struggling with the entirety of that value system. We don't veer from that value system from childhood very much, but we do have to make it our own. We have to take those values that are linked to judgments and make them our own. How are we going to internalize that value system and make it something that's palatable to us, that makes us have courage to live a good life, a virtuous life, something that keeps us healthy rather than self-betrayal?

Mental and physical health issues are directly linked to your value system. Not having one or living one is self-betrayal of what your beliefs are. That's why you must cut yourself open and question. This is why you must identify your top two values, in measurable, observable terms. When you break them down or cut them open to see what they're about, this is health. Workplace wellness or illness, or illness as a role or as a function is directly linked to our values. An illness mentality is directly related to values and the greed of not identifying them. Listing them sometimes is really hard, but defining them in measurable terms is absolutely necessary for health. The word *valor* is strength of mind or spirit. Your mental health, your spiritual health, are of course directly related. Your physical health is extremely linked to your values. Do you have valor to live your values? This is personal bravery, nobody can tell you how to live your life or what your values are but yourself.

Valer in Spanish means to be of worth, to have worth. Where you put your money, your time, and your resources, which are the currency of the material world, shows me what you value. What you find to be worthy. You can be saying that you are not lazy. But if you're spending all your time scrolling on social media, not being productive, as you'd define it, then you are lazy and self-betraying. You're not valuing hard work or productivity. Where do you spend your time? Are there distractions? Are you spending it on unimportant tasks? Are you only responding to urgency? That's going to tell you a lot of what you value.

Why is it so hard for us to have a clear personal value system? We are not allowed to. In the childhood home, the coercive cult, the parents dictated the values, albeit they violated the values all the time. In our child mind, if we honor the good values they instilled in us, then we will be good girls and boys, and we will get a Costco-card version of love and needs. The reason it is hard to define our personal value system is because it is directly linked to our basic unmet needs.

If we identify our values, we are what I call *dethroning our parents*. Dethroning our parents simply means we will surpass their health; financial, mental, spiritual or physical. We will break through the limits they taught us so we can seek our ultimate potential in what we value. I call this is the *Plexiglass Paradox*. Plexiglass is thick, opaque, a bit cloudy; however, it's clear enough to know what is on the other side. On the other side of the limitations given to you at conception by your parents, is what you truly seek and what your soul came to accomplish. If you don't question your values and define them, you can never get on the other side of the plexiglass. We are afraid of dethroning our parents and seeking our own value system, for fear of not getting any of our needs met, so we stick with what we know: conditional love and shabby unmet needs appearing to be sufficient.

Unmet Needs

There are four unmet needs. The first is safety and security, the second is protection, the third is validation and the fourth is love. Safety and security is linked to coercion. Nobody had a safe childhood. You didn't know what was going to set your parents off. You didn't know if you were going to get in trouble for bringing home a B instead of an A. You didn't know exactly what to expect, and it was not directly related to you. You might have been given a "You need to get straight A's," or "You need to take out the trash on Tuesdays." You might have been given that sort of safety, but the problem is, this is where the narcissism comes in. If your mom or dad were having a bad day, they were set up, they got into a car accident, they got fired or something didn't go right for them, they would take it out on you, because your job is to meet their needs. All of a sudden, you internalized that life is not safe or secure. "*I must make it safe and secure for my parents, then I will be worthy, then I will be of value.*" This is directly related to why we will not have bravery, courage, or valor to assume our own needs and our own value system.

I often ask clients, what happens? What do you lose when you make yourself safe? When you make a safe world for yourself? What do you lose if you become healthy financially, spiritually, mentally, and sexually? There's a cost. What do you lose if you actually stand up for your values and define your values? What is it that you lose? You might lose your entire false identity, the masks you've gotten comfortable wearing. All you're refusing to lose is a conditional version of love, the Costco card membership to your family's definition of conditional love. I personally seek the Nordstrom's version of love: self-love, unconditional love towards myself and meeting my own needs. Because that's the way the family works; based on these secret motives, judgments or values that no one talks about, these mokitas.

Ask yourself, what do you give up? What do you lose when you actually take charge of life? When you become safe and secure? It's very scary. How much lack of safety and security there was, despite a loving home. Just not having structure, not having rules, not having open dialogue. Those things make us very unsafe. We don't want to lose. If you had a very physically unsafe, unhealthy childhood in terms of violence, you might be more likely to do this sort of interrogation. If your family seemed like an idyllic snow globe with small cracks or normal cracks, you may not go into deep self-analysis of this. Because, "*Well, it wasn't that bad!*" I can justify it and make excuses.

Carolyn said to me recently, "You know, sometimes people hear me talk to my mother and they say, Oh, you're so mean to her." Something that we struggle with during different ages of our life is how we speak to our parents. She's actually at a very appropriate age, twenty-one, to kind of push mom back and set a boundary, because her mom is so invasive. Later on, we might learn techniques for how to get out of the energy so that we're not so enmeshed. That comes with skill, time, and wisdom.

It's not unusual for people that don't have safety to have very enmeshed homes that they pull away from. This is the Neptune archetype; the pulling away and the boundary-setting is the Saturn archetype. It's not wrong or right, you could choose to separate from your parents, but at the end of the day, it's all in your head; that's why the eleven chocolate chips at work, mirroring back to you what is really happening in your psyche, always bring it back to yourself. It's about creating these boundaries, structures, and pillars in your head, not necessarily externally, although sometimes the external environment needs a very strict boundary to keep your parents or other relationships at bay; I call these *hard edges*. Especially if it was not safe. Asking what you lose, it seems sort of like an oxymoron, that we would lose something by standing up for ourselves. That we would lose something if we create safety, if we become healthy, but we do. We lose our story, we lose our identity. We might lose very key players in our life that are feeding into our unmet needs if we start meeting them for ourselves. Some people will swallow you, and there is no space for them in your life—absolutely have a hard edge, but then, bring it back to which archetype does this person represent, and where do you need a boundary in your life in regards to that theme?

When you embark on a journey of self-discovery, you may discover that you don't want health or need health. Life may not be that bad. The pain may be bearable or the pain is serving you. That's okay. Not everyone wants balance or eudaemonia. We may be attached to the story and it's serving us, so that's often why we don't define our values. If you do not know your values, you will self-betray and get sick. You may not get physically sick, unless your body can no longer carry the weight of your thoughts, but you will get mentally sick. You will burn out or get stressed. It's linked to self-betrayal, it's linked to not knowing who you are, and it's linked to not knowing your value system.

What are your top two values? How do your corporate values match up with your personal values? Are you working in a place that directly conflicts with or violates your value system? Are you in a fear-based culture because you can't confront things from childhood? You're just still in the story, creating the fight or flight. Is being sick or being the victim still serving you? What's your personal definition of health? It's going to be linked directly to work and money. Does the thread that you share with your job make you sick, or does it add to health in your life? You get to define health in your own terms. There are a few definitions of health, for instance, the World Health Organization states that "health is a state of complete physical, mental, and social well-being. Not merely the absence of disease or infirmity." They're talking about physical, mental, and social health as being a whole and complete person. The *Food for Thought Pyramid* defines health as play, relationships, prayer, balanced emotions, resilience, and exercise. Is health for you only physical? Is it spiritual? Is it emotional? Is it financial? You get to decide the pillars that you define as health. Ayurveda's definition of health is a balance of the physical components of the body, the mind, but adds the soul's component by saying health is established in Self. This is the individuation process, this is absolutely knowing your values, your worth, your identity, your purpose. This image represents some of the pillars of health that may be important according to your value system.

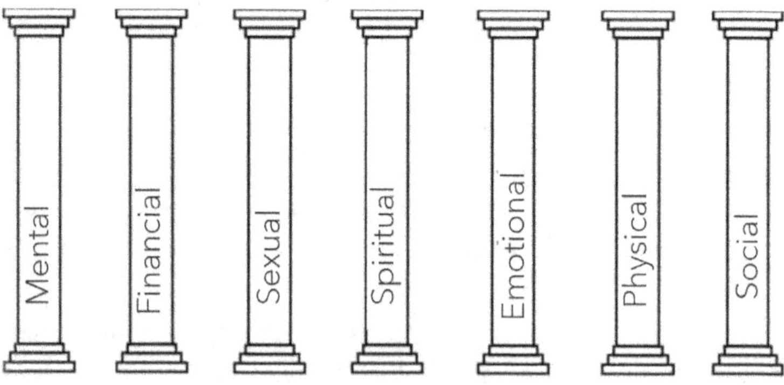

Examples of pillars of health in the individuation process. Identify your top two values and see how they support each individual pillar.

Fill them in and see if you're living up to your value system. The pillars of help make up your definition of health. This is again very personal, they're linked to your values. They're linked to your rulebook and philosophy of life, you cannot have a rulebook for life, or have a definition of health or philosophy of life if you don't know what pillars construct health in your mind. Maybe for you it's all about financial health and ambition, get very clear on what those are. The pillars here list financial, sexual, emotional, mental, spiritual, physical, and social. In my book *The Seven Gates*, I recommend to break up their rulebook into chunkable sections. The sections are going to be directly linked to your values and your judgments. Your values, your health, and your pillars are directly related your pillars of health defined by you. Get a notebook and divide your pillars of health that are linked to your value system and write your rules around that area of life, in measurable, observable terms. When you start defining your values, if you're brutally honest, you will discover you have bad bucket values and good bucket values. Bad bucket values are directly linked to what we deem wrong and unhealthy, like the deadly sins, vices, passions or thieves; however, we must identify two bad bucket values and two good bucket values to begin being whole.

The only way to stop the 0-100 swings of gluttonous, childlike thinking is to neutralize the swings, and identification with our shadow aspects, our darker values, is necessary. You may realize you're quite financially greedy; that's okay, two of the bad bucket values are permitted, as long as you define and measure them so you have a gauge up to what is enough. There is shame associated with having these earthly desires, and this shame keeps us from our spiritual selves. We were erroneously taught that we couldn't have earthly desires and be spiritual. The moment you have a judgement about someone, you've attached a bad bucket value to it, so instead of being shamed by the impure thought, link it back to the deadly sin or the vice and own it.

Brené Brown says, "The shame never goes away." The shame in her language is the impure thought in my language. That impure thought is directly linked to the bad bucket item you value. It's not about putting these away, but rather identifying that recognizing these aspects of yourself will lead to mental health, physical health, and spiritual health. Part of the coercive childhood trauma we experience is that our parents shamed us for the exact things they said not to do, but they did. Part of the inner work is realizing the incongruence in what we say and do, just like our parents. Rather than unveiling that our parents were incongruent, and questioning it, we take the good values at face value, all the while knowing they were hypocrites and doing one thing and saying another. Shame is created during zero to seven, and it is linked to our power currency. Once we unmask this realization, we start getting healthy.

Power Currency

Your first moment of shame establishes your power currency. It seems odd that the exact thing that created the shame becomes your source of power and how you will shame others, but the subconscious only knows 0-100 thinking; therefore, the opposite is the same. When you identified the parent that had the power (the one creating the shame) you went seeking that power currency. Ironically, a parent you never knew or was absent, can often times be the parent with the power currency you seek. There are two power currencies: covert and overt. If your father had the money and was a yeller, or perhaps he hit you for coming home late, you identified this power currency as the one that shamed you, and the one that you'd use to shame others. It's a hard pill to swallow, but it's the dysfunction of the psychological homeostasis! Therefore, each time you make a judgement, this power currency appears, you shame yourself, and then you violate your value system and self-betray; all in an attempt to hide the bad bucket value or vice you associate with power. It's a sick, vicious cycle. The first step to health is to identify what you value, even if you deem it good or bad. Next, is to get clear on how you will live out those values. It's what feels right with you—what's your truth? That's spiritual work, that's mental health, that's living your value system. This is very personal, and it's your definition of health. Your judgments are confessions, and they're great. Your judgments are linked to values. What do you judge? If someone shows up and you don't like how they're looking, perhaps you value vanity, an Aphrodite archetype—that's okay. There's probably an incongruence from childhood around the value placed on vanity and image that you're trying to reconcile. By not owning the bad bucket value, by not clearly defining it in measurable and observable terms, you won't dethrone your parents. You'll keep a conditional version of love and you will self-betray and possibly get sick. Are you sick because you cannot tolerate a value system that you have? Below I list the deadly sins; however, in every tradition or philosophy, there is a version of the sins called vices, passions or thieves. Identify which you are judging in others; they're linked to your bad bucket values and need to be defined clearly.

Deadly Sins

Envy is very much linked to emotions. It's to do with melancholy and depression. There's a link psychologically to envy.

Lust is oftentimes linked to sexuality or coveting what someone else has.

Greed tends to be linked to material, often financial assets.

Pride. Pride has a lot to do with your mental health. Do you think you're better? Do you think you're smarter? Do you think you're so brilliant and nobody recognizes it? Do you play small in terms of your knowledge to not make people feel dumb?

Gluttony is most often linked to physical health; however, a gluttonous or a hoarding tendency doesn't only have to be food.

Wrath. Are you angry? Do you take it out on your relationships, your children, your friends, your family, your co-workers? Anger or wrath is definitely something that we typically have.

Sloth is oftentimes linked to spiritual laziness, more so than earthly laziness.

Virtue Ethics

Virtue ethics is an approach to ethics that takes the notion that virtue, conceived as excellence, is fundamental. Perfection is a child's script, perfection is an insecurity, a feeling of abandonment or low self-worth. Rather, strive for excellence. Virtue ethics is linked to virtues, to living an excellent life, and an excellent life must be defined by you and only you. In virtue ethics, they say that there are specific character traits that are linked to human flourishing, eudaemonia. The goddess Eudaemonia and workplace wellness is when you're in balance with self. When you're in balance looking at the archetypes of those around you, identifying what you judge is simply about yourself, and working through those judgements. You will flourish healthfully when you live these virtuous traits or have these character traits. You are the only one that can determine what those are.

Virtue ethics also says that the action must have an intrinsic value. This is not Kohlberg's conventional morality, *"I'm going to do this because someone is watching,"* like a good boy or good girl, but rather this is intrinsic. Nobody can tell me how I live, but I live according to my values. It has to be intrinsic, so the motivation is for Self, not external or an image of what societal conventions expect.

Deontology, another branch of ethics, is related more to duty and moral obligation. Deontologists believe there are ethics or values that you have to have based on moral obligation or duty to society. Virtue ethics is more about an inward philosophy, what you feel is right, what your definitions are, what your self-worth is; the way that you live your truth. Aristotle, who prescribed to virtue ethics, stated twelve top virtues: 1) Courage, 2) Temperance, 3) Liberality, 4) Magnificence, 5) Magnanimity, 6) Proper ambition, 7) Patience, 8) Truthfulness, 9) Wittiness, 10) Friendliness, 11) Modesty, and 12) Justice or righteous indignation. These are linked to the twelve archetypes.

Aristotle stated there was a golden mean between the extremes and deficiencies of these virtues. In *The Seven Gates*, I call this the forty-eight to fifty-two. The neutralizing swings of the zero to one hundred is the child script inherited at conception. Only when you define your values, in measurable terms, can you stop the zero-to-one-hundred swings, find the forty-eight to fifty-two, or golden mean, and create health and eudaemonia.

Aristotle said, "A life of happiness is a life of excellent functioning." Again, it's about excellence defined by you intrinsically, not another. It's not related to perfection; rather, the forty-eight to fifty-two midpoint. A life of virtue is a life in which the rational faculties are in control. This goes back to emotional health. If your emotions are out of control, if emotional swings dictate behavior and you're reactive in a zero-to-one-hundred fashion, then you're not equanimous, you're not in a state of balance or health. You can't think rationally to make a choice. With Aristotle, when your rational faculties are in control, when you actually stop to take a breath from the emotional swings, think, *"I get to choose,"* then you're living a life of virtue. Even if you choose to return back to the story, the drama and the child script, it's based on rational choice and free will. It's only when you're living in the forty-eight to fifty-two that life is virtuous.

Aristotle says that virtues are destroyed by excess, those zero-to-a-hundred swings. He says there isn't virtue in the swings, rather, you're living in vice, which then leads to judgments, impure thoughts, shame, self-betrayal and illness. A book called *CSV: Character Strengths and Virtues* was written by Christopher Peterson and Martin Seligman, in which they attempt to present a measure of humanist ideals of virtue, particularly six classes of virtue and twenty-eight character strengths. Similar to Aristotle, they include 1) Wisdom & Knowledge, 2) Courage, 3) Humanity, 4) Justice, 5) Temperance and 6) Transcendence. Again, it's related to values and the way you show up, that valor and that courage.

The Stoics believed in four cardinal virtues: 1) Prudence, 2) Justice, 3) Fortitude, and 4) Temperance. Again, balance, equanimity, stability and constancy are the virtues that balance your vices or deadly sins; however, you need both, bad bucket and good bucket, to be a whole person. It's all about the golden mean. The word *cardinal* means hinge. In many spiritual traditions, we use the word cardinal to indicate the directions or areas we need to find temperance. In Shamanism, when we open sacred space, which is to eliminate fear, shame, guilt and doubt, we call in the cardinal directions. In astrology, the hardest planetary placements, affecting the psyche, are those in cardinal placements. They're what keep us on edge, hinging, trying to find balance. They're linked to the liminal spaces and transitions in our life.

Work is a sacred space, a liminal space, where we hinge between our earthly and our spiritual selves, finding balance, the perfect alchemy between the two, and using all situations to help refine ourselves from lead to gold. Spirit and matter meet here, and work is so transitory in the sense that every day we need to figure out how to show up. You're going to test the waters, you're going to see. Can I push this a little further? Should I pull back? Was I too overly ambitious? Do I have to pull back? Was I reprimanded? How do I self-appraise? It's a constant self-appraisal, so we're constantly on the hinge. We're constantly in the transition, in that liminal space of how much, how little. How do I dip my toe or how do I pull back?

Cardinal means of the *greatest importance, fundamental*. It is of the greatest importance and fundamental that we discover the midpoint between our vices and virtues, our material selves and spiritual selves, and between ourselves and others. There isn't a precise point, an exactitude; it's a trial and error daily. This is partly what makes us feel so unsafe or insecure. Life is ambiguous, there's no control or black and white; however, the tenets laid out in a workspace environment are the best mirrors on how to live our lives. The glyph of the sun is simply a circle with a dot in the middle. It looks like a bullseye. The sun or the solar energy is the energy that provides life each day. This glyph represents the hero archetype. In astrology, the sun glyph represents you, the hero of your life, and you're in the center of the solar system. The glyph indicates original sin, which simply means, missing the mark. The fact that we're humans means we miss the mark, we're never going to have perfection, we are always a little to the left, a little to the right, trying to find the forty-eight to fifty-two or the golden mean. We strive for excellence, and excellence is this midpoint; however, it is personal. What is the midpoint for me? What is virtuous for me? What are values for me? What is health for me? What are my pillars? What are the definitions for me to be safe for my life, in my psyche, in my world, financially, sexually, spiritually, mentally, and emotionally?

The sun glyph representing the solar archetype.

Another Aristotelian archetype is excess balanced by the concept of deficiency. Deficiencies are zero, while excesses are one hundred. Since Aristotle said that excess kills virtue, and virtue is where you hit the mark. Again there's no precision, this is very personal to you, find the range that works for you, I prefer the forty-eight to fifty-two mark; however, it may be thirty to forty, or sixty to seventy. It's personal, but then define the values in measurable and observable terms to live according to that range, which is equanimity for you.

VICE (Miss the mark)	VIRTUE (Hit the mark)	VICE (Miss the mark)
DEFICIENCY	**BALANCE**	**EXCESS**
COWARDICE	COURAGE	RASHNESS
LAZINESS	DETERMINATION	GREED
COMBATIVENESS	FRIENDLINESS	FLATTERY
STINGINESS	GENEROSITY	WASTEFULNESS
RUTHLESSNESS	MERCY	SELF-SUBJUGATION
IRRITABILITY	PATIENCE	APATHY
IMPULSIVENESS	SELF-CONTROL	INDECISIVENESS
MEEKNESS	SELF-LOVE	ARROGANCE
SHADINESS	TRANSPARENCY	TMI (TOO MUCH INFO)
HUMORLESSNESS	WITTINESS	ABSURDITY

The zero to one-hundred using Aristotle's vices and virtues.

Omphalos means the navel, the center or the hub of something. In Greek mythology it represented a stone at Delphi considered the naval of the earth and looks like the sun glyph. It was believed that Delphi was the center of the world and all prophecies happened at the Oracle at Delphi, which had a sign at the entrance, *Man Know Thyself.* We need to become the center of our life, the only way that we can become the center, the navel, the omphalos is by knowing ourselves. Our belly button is our navel, and we are fed through it during pregnancy. Our mother gave us breath and gave us food and nourishment during that time in which we transitioned into the earth. That was it; we don't owe anything past that. We have to come and find our own path. Be the center of our own life. It's very difficult, this is why people will not write down their values or define them clearly.

All earthly experiences are spiritual experiences. The mother earth symbolism is connected with fecundity, birth, impregnation, and birth. Like Virgo, the materia prima is the land where the seed of your divinity is housed. They have a cosmic structure. All things bring you back to this center, the belly button, the navel. You being the center of your world, you knowing yourself are spiritual experiences taking place in the material body. Every single thing is a spiritual experience when it brings you back to your individuation process. It brings you back to your values. It brings you back to your worth. How you're going to manage your money, your time, and resources are the language and the currency of the earthly world.

The omphalos was also a stone given to Saturn or Cronos. The symbolism is that in order to know ourselves and be the center or our lives, we must use Saturn lessons of limitations, boundaries, flexibility and humility. Boundaries are all mother earth, are all symbolic, are the form that houses this divinity. That houses our center of self, our fire, so that it can grow appropriately and not burn. Prophecy is a Greek value but also a curse. If you live according to what you were prophesized to be, like many of the Greek gods, you will die a fateful death; however, if you maintain being the center of your life, the solar energy, you can use others to inform where you need to grow and change.

At the Oracle at Delphi, it states, "Man know thyself and you will know the wonders of the universe." The Universe is within, represented by the twelve archetypes, the twelve planets and asteroids, represented by the twelve disciples and the twelve Olympian gods, however you want to look at it. It is said that Zeus sent two eagles, the symbol of transformation and the shadow rising out of the impure thoughts. Rising like the phoenix, the eagles another symbol of that same message to find the center of the world. It was said that the stone, the omphalos, was thrown and dropped at Delphi. You are the center of your world, your values, your shadow, your impure thoughts; owning them and transmuting them. Nobody else!

The Torah, in Judaism, is the law of God as revealed to Moses and recorded in the first five books of the Hebrew scriptures, the *Pentateuch*. In the Hebrew tradition, they read a weekly Torah portion. The fourth weekly Torah portion of the annual Jewish cycle or Torah reading, Genesis 18:1-22:24 is called *Parashat Vayera* and means "He appeared," and can mean teaching, guidance and direction. When working with clients, or listening archetypally to see what a situation is providing for me to work on, I listen for "the first words" because they speak to the direction in which the psyche is being led by them and gives me insight to the guidance I need. In every creation myth, there's an intact universal consciousness. In the Bible it states, "In the beginning was the word," and then it says, "The word was God." When I start a session, I listen to the first words the client says. When you start to listen archetypally and symbolically, you start to pay attention to more than the earthly consciousness, how you're tapping into the universal consciousness, and you become the mystic. Those first few words spoken in any conversation are going to link you to the archetype or the issue that the person must work through, and again, what you need to learn as well. This is linked to a value system that needs clarity or a bad bucket value they're judging.

Kerry was sharing a story about her daughter in cheerleading camp and how she was tired of spending money if her daughter was not very good. Money conversations are linked to the archetype of Saturn, indicating there is a greed value that she needs to reconcile, a limit or a boundary that is needed in her life, and a self-worth issue. The session now has a form, because the client has indicated where the session needs to go. In return, I now know I also need to see where she is mirroring my own issues in these areas. That archetype shows up to say, "I want to address this," so we must start listening archetypally, rather than materially.

Archetypes

In the *Chocolate Chip Theory of Leadership*, there is one chocolate chip representing you; however, on the other side mirroring you, there are eleven chocolate chips. These chocolate chips are symbolic of the archetypes that are fragments of your psyche, often unintegrated, and they cause problems. Since we've identified that anything you judge or dislike in another is a mirror of yourself, the archetypes are the patterns found in all persons and represent the twelve chocolate chips. Identifying the archetypes in the people that annoy you gives you a clear shadow aspect of your psyche that you're not identifying in yourself as problematic, therefore, you are projecting onto others. The archetypes are twelve; however, no matter how you number or name them, these are the traits that every human being possesses as their psyche's structure.

I prefer to use the Greek gods and goddesses, mainly the Olympians, which teach you what story you're living out at work and is directly related to your role in the family, parenting style, unmet needs and shadow aspects of the inner child that will show up in these archetypes. You'll notice the different gods and goddesses have overlaps, but the twelve archetypes are the same twelve archetypes over and over again.

Archetypes in *The Office*

Because the office is such a prime place for seeing all archetypes, the hit TV show *The Office* is a great place to discuss the twelve archetypes, which are in each one of us, and the twelve chocolate chips mentioned in the *Chocolate*

Chip Theory of Leadership, not only represent the colleagues, but the aspects of you that you cannot see without a mirror.

Archetype	Greek Mythology	*The Office*	Description
Hero	Apollo	Jim	This is you as the hero of your story. You're the sun, it's all about you. It is very important that we understand the archetype because there tends to be a narcissistic trend to this archetype. If it's all about us and we're the divine, what we're trying to do is obviously manage our fire in one direction or another, but we either play small, or we can scourge another in the process; neither is balanced. The shadow aspect of the sun is the darkness: what are you hiding behind your light? You're hiding the deadly sin or vices and afraid that someone will figure you out.
Caregiver	Artemis, Demeter	Phyllis	The caregiver is the moon and the mother archetype. The moon has to do with the mother, there's a very passive-aggressive codependent tendency. Like the moon changes its face every day, so does this archetype. You'll change your face to become whatever the other needs, so you can get your needs met. They put the needs of others before their own, but it isn't genuine. The shadow aspect of the caregiver is staying a child, and the belief that if I meet your needs, maybe my needs from childhood will finally be met. There's a lack of self-worth in this archetype and childhood wounding.

Archetype	Greek Mythology	*The Office*	Description
Jester	Mercury, Hermes	Michael	The jester is Michael in *The Office*, the class clown or the office clown. They might be very good communicators and negotiators because it is Mercury in Greek mythology, the messenger of the gods. Yet they might also be the buffoon; they don't know the timing to make a joke or can't read the room and when it is not appropriate. The shadow side of this archetype is the need for validation and feeling intellectually inferior or superior.
Creator	Ares	Andy	The creator archetype has to do with competition and this person wants the next rung of the ladder, continuously. There's a big ambitious streak here and maybe we'll bulldoze those ahead of us to get ahead. In Greek mythology, it is Ares, and they tend to have a bit of a temper or anger issues. The shadow aspect is the unprocessed anger from childhood for having his boundaries repeatedly violated. If the creator can be competitive, physically strong and show anger, his boundaries won't be messed with again.
Lover	Venus, Aphrodite	Kelly	The lover is Venus or Aphrodite in Greek mythology. In *The Office*, this archetype is represented by Kelly. Makeup, Instagram, the social butterfly at the low-consciousness level are her priorities. This archetype has a strong focus on relationships and wanting to be liked. Being heard in relationships and social interactions in the office is a critical theme of this archetype. The vanity of the lover archetype is the shadow aspect believing she is only worthy when her image is socially acceptable. Her self-worth is contingent on what others see.

Archetype	Greek Mythology	*The Office*	Description
Ruler	Lilith	Meredith	The ruler archetype is someone who has big ideas but it's to meet their own needs. They may cheat and love to party. This archetype can be vulgar, curse a lot at the low-level consciousness and create drama as a negative attention-seeking behavior. The shadow archetype is the prostitute, trying to be the seductress or scandalous so her low self-worth will never be on actual display. The scandalous behavior is to cover inadequacy and severe low self-esteem.
Sage	Saturn, Cronus	Dwight	The sage is the Saturn or senex archetype from Greek mythology. They are the rule-keeper, the one that has the structure, that has to manage the office policies and procedures. They are the shadow archetype of the control freak. They're obsessed with details and procedures so they can control everything. The fear is being dispensable and found out that they don't contribute much because they're inadequate and easily replaced.
Rebel, Revolutionary	Uranus	Creed	The revolutionary in *The Office* is Creed. This archetype makes their own rules, always wants to be original, and they want to beat to their own drum. They get very caught up in ideals. In Greek mythology, it's Uranus. The shadow of the rebel is to create chaos and drama so that the real insignificance he feels is never noticed. They fail to have structure and plans and sell it as freedom.

Archetype	Greek Mythology	*The Office*	Description
Innocent	Neptune, Poseidon	Stanley	We all have an innocent archetype, because we are trying to reclaim our child script, via a victim, from childhood. The innocent in the office tries to people-please, but the shadow is that they might avoid responsibility by playing small or playing childlike. The shadow aspects are victim, martyr, rescuer, and acting naïve so others take care of them while they manipulate with their covert power.
Magician	Pluto, Hades	Ryan	The magician is the loner archetype and tends to have a before and an after, as if two people. Ryan in *The Office* comes back to the office and he has two different roles. They tend to be visionaries and have big plans; however, they can create crisis and a lot of drama. They're always in in conflict, like a tortured soul. The shadow aspect of the magician is acting dark and unavailable because they were outcast as broken or demonic, when in reality they see the truth of things and rather than own it, they self-deprecate to feel they fit in with humanity.
Everyman	Chiron	Angela	The every person is the commoner, it could be the wounded warrior, it could be someone that tries to patch up things. He wants to be kind, they might be very empathic, but really what motivates them is the caregiver. This is Chiron in Greek mythology, half-human, half-animal. The shadow aspect is illness or OCD and needing to purify and clean everything. They don't feel there's anything special about them so they sell a nun archetype so they feel superior to hide the inferiority.

Archetype	Greek Mythology	*The Office*	Description
Explorer	Jupiter, Zeus	Jan	The explorer is always ready to move. He doesn't really get hung up on things because he's always planning the "next thing." The shadow is the glutton and the escape artist. There's very little follow through and although they tend to have positions or power and appear wise, they're foolish and lack discernment.

Your words are linked to your values, your values are linked to your archetypes. Integrating your archetypes is key to making you whole. Here are all the archetypes with you as the hero, you're the sun in the center. What bothers you or rubs you the wrong way is how to identify that that archetype is one that you need to work on.

If you link it back to the vices, to the virtues, to your judgments, you're going to start seeing this threaded in your life; it might be an area that is blatantly obvious, but nobody tells you about. Maybe people have criticized you, or even a self-appraisal or an appraisal at work has come up and you're appalled that would be something that someone would describe you as. Remember, a lot of these shadow aspects are hidden. We hide them in those zero-to-one-hundred swings, because we don't want to be like our parents. You can see which aspects are linked to the bad buckets, are linked to those shadow aspects of parents, and are linked to values that your parents said, "No that's not the way we are in this house," but then broke their own rules in other circumstances.

Joseph Campbell said, "If you really want to help this world, what you will have to teach is how to live in it." We are not taught how to live a full, whole life. We're given threads, we're given fragments of this teaching in childhood. Our parents give us our consciousness, our values, our thoughts, and we must put it all together in a meaningful way; however, the answer is in your story.

Sacred space is everywhere you are, if you're living truth. Live truth and teach your truth. Teach people how to live comfortably with both their bad bucket and good bucket values. When you have a clear value system, you will not self-betray. You can live safely in the world. Teach people to embrace all aspects of themselves, even the shadow side—especially the shadow side. All of those archetypes that perhaps are competitive voices that you don't like about yourself or that you judge in others are in you; embrace them into wholeness. Judgments are simply aspects of yourself that need discovery.

Teach people that they're every person. In spiritual philosophy, there is no other, we are all one. Anything that you don't like about someone is in you. Listen to what other people say; the universe is speaking through them, plus they're showing aspects of ourselves that we want to integrate. It's important to learn how to use their money, time, and resources wisely. Learning to use our resources or our time and saying no. Having the valor and the courage to start and end meetings on time, respects you and others. Being a no sayer is really a helpful tool for living. Teach people to make themselves a priority by making yourself a priority. You're ultimately the sun, the navel of your solar system, of your life; it's all about you. Then and only then can you give and serve to another.

Teach people how to have structure and limits in this day and age of independence, originality and individuation. We think that it's about creating chaos and not having any structure or limits, when actually boundaries are the safest and the healthiest way to really be original and shine. The oppressor is in your head, namely, from childhood. Limits and boundaries are safe, and will create an environment for your divinity to shine through your humanity. Teach people how to have a personal rulebook and a philosophy of life that's rooted in their definition of health, in their value system linked to themselves. Take your story and create a vision for your life from what was missing in your story. You're the research question, and your story has the answer. Spread the message, it's a universal one.

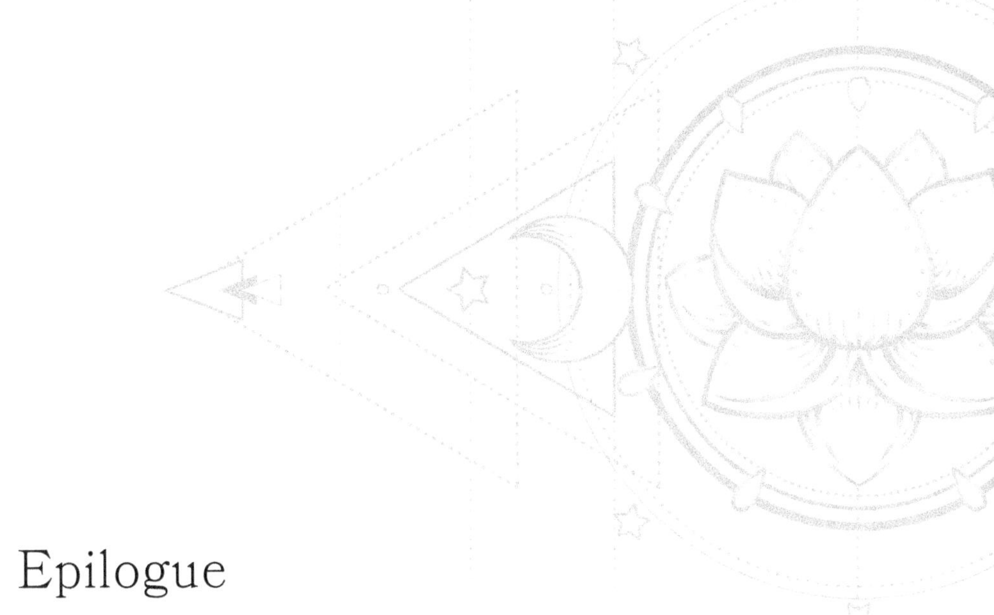

Epilogue

The point of this book has been to encourage you to connect to the universal consciousness while you spend hours at work in your earthly consciousness, using the universal law, the Principle of Correspondence, *as within, so without*, to navigate both states of consciousness, leading you to wholeness.

Using the Saturn archetype in a balanced way, you can learn to love yourself unconditionally, meet your own needs, avoid illness, manage your time, money and resources appropriately, say no and define your values, while still learning humility, suppleness, and exerting appropriate authority.

Liminal spaces are spaces where both states of consciousness, spirit and matter, appear and teach us all spaces are sacred and become opportunities to become content and achieve wholeness. Workspaces resemble the family childhood spaces and are opportunities to heal wounds from childhood and move away from coercive parenting or leadership techniques and rather show up for ourselves.

The enneagram shows us how to identify our role in the organization and what our inner child needs to heal. The *Chocolate Chip Theory of Leadership* represents all the archetypes found in your psyche that need integrating, and are extrapolated to the characters you will meet along your professional path. Use them as mirrors to heal earthly relationships as well as subconscious wounds that began at conception.

The models presented in this book are to dethrone anyone and anything that takes your power, consciously or unconsciously, so that you can be the leader of your life. May you find the balance between the ordinary and the mystical in all.

Dethroning Sacred Spaces
Workbook

Worksheet 1: Using Saturn's Limitations to Grow

1. List five qualities where you excel. List five qualities where you can learn to bend and be supple and learn from others. Who in your office displays the five qualities you'd like to incorporate.

2. Skinny cow years are listed below. Can you identify what happened in each of those years, as well as you can remember, and identify a theme that you may be repeating that is here to teach you a lesson?

3. Have you dethroned limiting beliefs your parents imposed on you? What limitation did they give you? We all got a limitation on how happy, successful, rich, healthy, powerful or in love we could be. What did they say? Where were they hipocrites in their own life around this?

Worksheet 2: Personal TED talk

Engage in a daily personal TED talk and answer these questions.

- Pick a situation that created conflict.
- What number was it on a scale of 1 to 10?
- Who did it represent? Something mother or father would do?
- What didn't you like about it? Can you link this to something you've done in the past, currently do or are capable of doing in the future?
- What deadly sin or vice could you link it to?
- When this conflict occurs what does it negatively prove about you?
- Could you name this emotion? Where do you feel this in the body?

The Personal TED talk synopsis.

1. Is the conflict representative of mother or father? (THOUGHT inherited at conception is limiting and impure.)
2. What don't I like about the conflict? (This is linked to a DESIRE/ flawed body and a judgement I make about myself that I'm projecting onto the other.)
3. What does it prove about me when I create this conflict? (EMOTION I have to feel in order to convince myself I'm human and part of the human race/my family.)

Who is its mother or father? What don't I like about it? What does it prove about me?

Worksheet 3: Sphere of Consciousness Worksheet

When something negative arises in your life, can you link it to a vice or deadly sin?

How did your parents live this out? One parent usually lives out one extreme and the other parent usually lives out the other extreme. For instance, the car breaks down, mom may get angry while dad protends nothing is wrong. This is known as the 0 to 100.

Can you identify three criteria that would be a midpoint, the 48 to 52 (virtue), of what mom and dad would do? They need to be observable and measurable criteria.

VICE (Miss the mark)	VIRTUE (Hit the mark)	VICE (Miss the mark)
DEFICIENCY	**BALANCE**	**EXCESS**
COWARDICE	COURAGE	RASHNESS
LAZINESS	DETERMINATION	GREED
COMBATIVENESS	FRIENDLINESS	FLATTERY
STINGINESS	GENEROSITY	WASTEFULNESS
RUTHLESSNESS	MERCY	SELF-SUBJUGATION
IRRITABILITY	PATIENCE	APATHY
IMPULSIVENESS	SELF-CONTROL	INDECISIVENESS
MEEKNESS	SELF-LOVE	ARROGANCE
SHADINESS	TRANSPARENCY	TMI (TOO MUCH INFO)
HUMORLESSNESS	WITTINESS	ABSURDITY

Worksheet 4: Heiros Gamos Worksheet; Mission & Vision

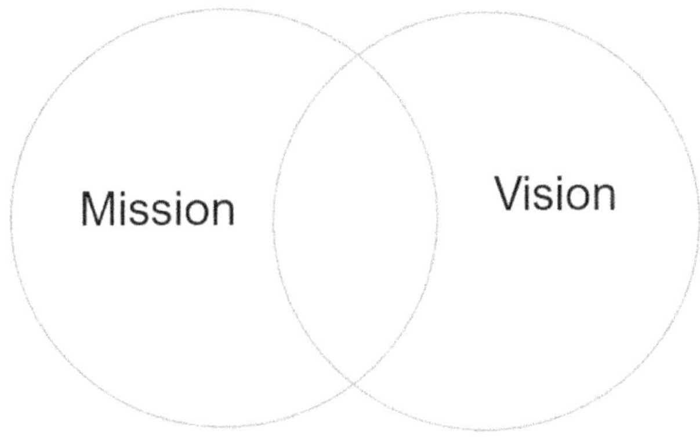

Write your mission statement for life.

Write your vision statement for life.

How does your corporate mission and vision statement support you achieveing your mission and vision for your life?

What is the one thread that brings you to work everyday. A paycheck is fin; however, can you find another one?

What is an absolute non-negotiable that if your employer asked you to do, without a doubt, would cause you to immediately resign?

What unmet need does your job fulfill? It's usually safety/security, protection or validation, but it can be others.

How do you use the mission of the job and the people that you work with to make your life purpose-driven?

Worksheet 5: Leadership Wheel

Label your wheel with 12 slices.

What 12 qualities must you have as a leader?

You can use the one provided below. List a light aspect and a shadow aspect you have linked to each of the twelve qualities.

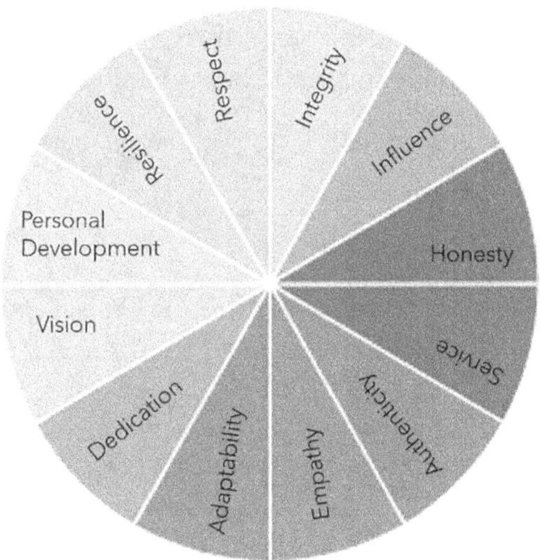

Vision. How do you see yourself? What's your role in the organization? What are your expectations around this job?

Dedication: Again, your values. What do you buy into? What incongruences are there between your values and the organization's values? Do they overlap? Are they self-serving? Are they self-betraying? Do they violate your nonnegotiables? Do you value yourself? If you value yourself, then how are you going to show up with your time, your money, and your resources? Are you going to ask for the appropriate salary, or will you cower when that conversation comes up? Are you going to ask for raises, are you going to leave when it's time to leave? Unless, of course, there's some big event that you need to prepare for. Are you going to honor your values?

Adaptability: This has to be with thoughts, and you're going to use the workplace to allow others to mirror to you your impure thoughts and the way you think about yourself.

Empathy: Are your needs met through this job? You must meet your needs; that's your responsibility. Is the job helping you to see your thoughts and meet your own needs?

Authenticity: Are you of value to your employer? Do you show up as yourself, balanced, or are you one of those people that morphs with whatever they need? Do you put people on a pedestal? Do you view yourself as authentic and show up balanced in life?

Service: Are you a container for the mission and the vision of the organization? Again, you've got to check the mission and the vision. Does this align with your values? Do you like the mission and the vision?

Honesty: Do you contribute honestly? Do you promote the values of the organization or are you embarrassed? Do you lie, or cower at the idea of anyone knowing that you worked there?

Influence: Are you making a difference? Do you have a position of influence? Not necessarily in the organization, but do you feel that you're an influential member of the team? Do you model the values of the organization in your personal life? Would the same person in your personal and your professional life have the same value system?

Integrity: Again, are your personal values and the organization in alignment? Because that would be truth.

Respect: Do you spread the mission? You have to believe in something to spread it.

Resilience: Do you knock down negativity with clear communication? This does not mean put on a smile, everything's great, positive vibes only. That is not what I'm about at all. It's, do we clear the air, do we talk about the mokitas, the elephant in the room, through clear communication?

Personal Development: Are you in union with the organization? Does this spiritually serve you? Does it serve the community? I told you that astrologically, we bring ourselves in individually in our work life. Over here in this personal sector, we work through spirituality with our material and spiritual parts. Then we go out into the community and become social beings, influential people withs vocations who give back to society. If the employer is not serving you, a whole person, then how are you going to give back to the community? You're still sort of down here, getting basic needs met because you're in a fear-based culture.

Worksheet 6: Pillars of Health

Identify your pillars of health. You can use the ones provided below. Identify at least one measurable, observable way you honor each pillar.

Is being sick or being the victim still serving you?

What's your personal definition of health?

Does the thread that you share with your job make you sick, or does it add to health in your life?

Is health for you only physical? Is it spiritual? Is it emotional? Is it financial? You get to decide the pillars that you define as health.

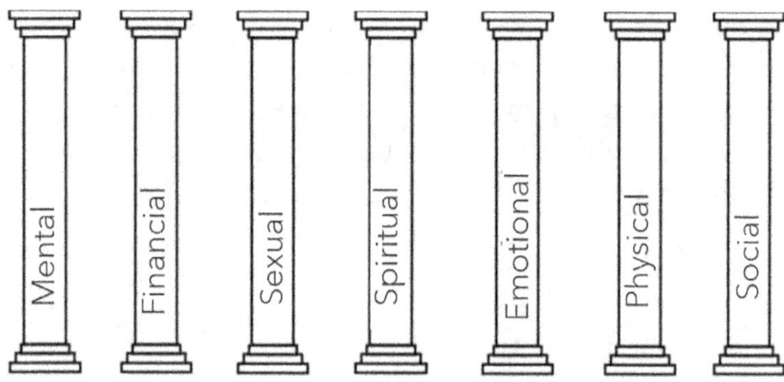

Fill the pillars in the way you wish to see the pillars of health, use as many or as few as you wish. Use these, or make your own. and see if you're living up to your value system. The pillars help make up your definition of health. This is again very personal, they're linked to your values. They're linked to your rulebook and philosophy of life, you cannot have a rulebook for life, or have a definition of health or philosophy of life if you don't know what pillars construct health in your mind. Maybe for you it's all about financial health and ambition, get very clear on what those are.

Worksheet 7: Values

What are your top two values (and it cannot be family)?

For each value list 3 observable and measurable ways you live true to those values.

Are there ways you self-betray those values?

What are your top two values? How do your corporate values match up with your personal values? Are you working in a place that directly conflicts with or violates your value system?

Worksheet 8: No Sayer & Board of Deflectors Worksheet

What is one thing that if occurred in your office you would be a no-sayer about?

Is it linked to your values?

Non-negotiables?

Are you willing to lose your job to speak out?

Can you say no to a project, a meeting a lunch invite you're not really feeling and will take time away from your real priorities?

Why do you say yes? Is it to be liked? Get validated?

Whay is it hard to say no? Who is it hard to say no to? Why?

Worksheet 9: Power Currency

What is the first moment of shame you can remember between the ages of 0 to 7? (It usually involves a parent, but anyone will do)

Did they use overt power like yelling, hitting, screaming or covert power like manipulation, passive-aggressive, gasligting or silent treatment?

How do you use that power currency in your work environment? How can you incorporate the other power currency?

Worksheet 10: Enneagram

What year did your company begin (open its door, go public, get incorporated)?

What year did you begin work at your organization?

Take the year they began-year you began and add a one. Reduce that number to a number between 1 and 9 by adding the four digits of the year togther.

Example: I started working at one employer in 2004. They opened in 1994. That's 10 + 1 = 11. 1+ 1 = 2. I'm working through 2 themes in that job which are harmony and conflict.

Identify what number you're working through at your current employment and how you're learning about the themes.

- Year One: New Beginning
- Year Two: Harmony & Conflict
- Year Three: Communication
- Year Four: Construction
- Year Five: Growth
- Year Six: Service, Health & Illness
- Year Seven: Introspection
- Year Eight: Power & Money
- Year Nine: Endings, Downsizing

How can you work on your shadow aspect?

Using the enneagram to know what aspect of your spiritual life you're there to work on has to do with identifying the unresolved emotions and desires linked to your limiting thoughts. Each number has a shadow aspect which includes an energetic or emotional component that robs our power. They are listed below:

- Year One: Resentment & Anger
- Year Two: Flattery & Pride
- Year Three: Vanity & Deceit
- Year Four: Melancholy & Envy
- Year Five: Avarice & Greed
- Year Six: Cowardice & Fear
- Year Seven: Opportunism & Gluttony
- Year Eight: Vengeance & Lust
- Year Nine: Indolence & Sloth

Worksheet 11: Ritual & Ceremony

What are some rituals at work?

How do you play at work?

Worksheet 12: Stress & Burnout

Do you have stress or burnout?

Stress is linked to tribal narcissism and burnout is linked to transcendental narcissism. Which one are you?

If you're a tribal narcissist, how can you add More spiritual awareness?

If you're a transcendental narcissist, how can you add More material awareness?

Do you get sick? What physical ailments do you suffer from from?

What's the function of that body part? What can the body be telling you about your psyche? Mind? Archetypes?

Worksheet 13: Limitations

What limitations do you feel your employer imposes on you?

Can they serve a function at all?

Where do you wish you were totally free and had no limits?

What chaos would that bring if you didn't have those limits?

Worksheet 14: Reverence

What one practice do you engage in (anywhere in your life) with reverence?

Can you do something similar at work? Just one thing?

Worksheet 15: What Defines You

Where do you think that form defines you?

Body image, money, material possessions, corner office?

Who are you without this in your life?

Worksheet 16: 5 Tenets of Being Zen

Where can you do one of these each day in your workspace?

1. *Take joy in service.*
2. *Treat each thing as the body of the Buddha.*
3. *Refuse judgments and preferences.*
4. *Do the best job that you can*
5. *Become one with your activity*

Worksheet 17: Conformity & Compliance

Conformity involves a request—someone requesting you do something, going along with people of equal status, and relies on the need to be socially accepted. Obedience is something you're told to do, involves an order, and is usually from somebody of a higher rank. It relies on social power.

Compliance is changing your behavior at the request of another person.

Where do you conform?

Where do you obey?

Where do you comply?

Worksheet 18: Qualities of a Great Boss and Employee

Where do you have these?

Where do you fall short?

What about your supervisor?

What is it mirroring in you?

Ten Qualities of a Great Employee and a Great Boss

1. He or she communicates a clear vision and connects the vision to daily tasks. This is clarity: to set clear expectations.
2. Provides feedback in coaching and perhaps in what you did wrong so you too can grow in a leadership position, if it's something what you want.
3. Someone who cares about the employee and may share personal experiences.
4. Team development.
5. Values employee perspective, your authenticity in the way that you show up in the employee attributes.
6. Ambitious.
7. Autonomous.
8. Confident.
9. Reliable.
10. Eager.

Worksheet 19: Chocolate Chip Theory
of Leadership Worksheet

Who are your 11 chocolate chips in your life? What do they show you about yourself? Identify your solar qualities like you did in worksheet one. Identify each of the remaining 11 archetypes and name a coworker for each archetype. What do they mirror in you that you cannot see clearly in yourself?

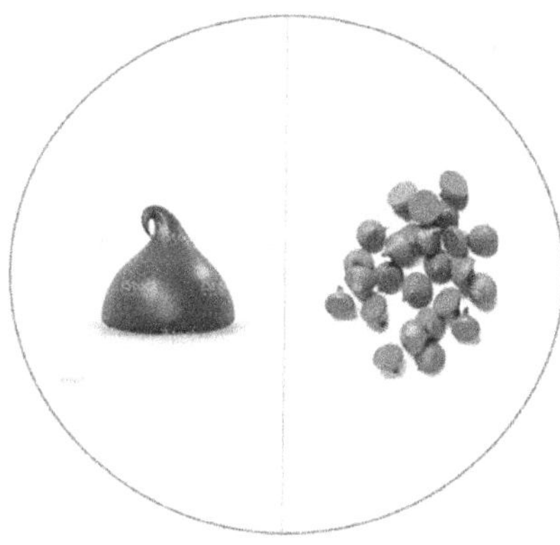

Worksheet 20: Dethroning the CEO & the COO

Do you spend 50% of your time, money and resources on yourself? If not, where are you wasting this energy?

Where are you ordinary at work?

Where are you original at work?

Do you create chaos and drama as a way to stay original?

Worksheet 21: Stone Soup

Are you being fed and nurtured at work? If so how, by whom?

Are you feeding and nurturing others? How and who?

Worksheet 22: Family of Origin

What was your origin story at your office? How'd you meet? Get the job?

What was the first "fight"? Crack in the snowglobe?

How des it resemble your childhood home?

What mokitas exist at the workplace that no one talks about?

What parenting style do they have at work: authoritative (tender teacher), authoritarian (rigid ruler) or permissive? What would you change?

Is your job psychologically safe?

Are you in a fear-based culture because you can't confront things from childhood?

Worksheet 23: Inner Child Wound

What is your enneagram number at work?

Find the inner child wound below with that number.

How can you help heal him or her?

1. Perfectionist	Intolerant
2. Obsessed	Fixated
3. Ruthless	Deception
4. Self-loathing	Low self-esteem
5. Withdrawn, disconnected	Psychotic
6. Confusion, contradictory	Chaotic
7. Excess, addiction	Suicide
8. Attention, hard-heart	Violent & destructive
9. Numb	Denial

How can the inner child integrate one of these light aspects?

- One: Serenity
- Two: Humility
- Three: Authenticity & Truthfulness
- Four: Balance & Equanimity
- Five: Detachment
- Six: Courage
- Seven: Sobriety
- Eight: Innocence; Purity of Thought
- Nine: Action

How can you have a fun time with your inner child with the numbered activities below:

One	Wants attention. Take her out for a solo date.
Two	Wants a play date with friends.
Three	Wants to be read to. Get a children's book, a favorite from childhood maybe, and read it to him/her.
Four	Wants structure and rules. Give her a strict bedtime or a strict routine in one small thing in life. Nothing too strict.
Five	Wants to have fun and get dirty. Get playdoh and get messy. Plant something. Fingerpaint.
Six	Wants some work. Wants to build something and see her work displayed on the fridge or on the mantle. For example, Build-A-Bear, a popsicle project a Lego project.
Seven	Wants quiet and solitude. Take a bubble bath or go for a walk, alone.
Eight	Wants to spend money. Buy her/him something frivolous, just because.
Nine	Wants to end something. Throw away some old clothes or old books or burn old journals. Do not donate it. It needs to clearly end by throwing it away, not passing it down to others.

Worksheet 24: Five C's of Diamond Leadership

Cut. What do you want to look like after the process of this job, of taking this job? When you take on the job, what is it that you want to look like afterwards? What are you going to purify? What are you going to carve away? What are you going to be chipping away at during this job? What's that going to make you look like after the process? Why are you working in a place? What is it that you're going to work through? After this job ends, in a week, two weeks, three years or thirty years, it doesn't matter, how will you improve as a result of this job?

Color. What are you thinking? What are your emotions? What are your desires? According to this, what are you judging? How can the job help you be more authentic, perhaps? What can you learn from those archetypes that you dislike or the elements you dislike?

Clarity. How can you forgive your imperfections at work? What zig when others are zagging can you bring to the job, to the role into the organization? How do those quirks and differences benefit the organization? How can you be you?

Carat. Are you honoring your time, money, and resources? Are you overworking for needs of validation, of morphing in not knowing how to say no, of coercion? You have to look at those things. Are you overdoing the workload?

Consciousness. Are you using the job to grow spiritually? Are you looking at the parallels from your snow globe from your unmet needs, from the parenting style, from coercion, from comparison, from your wound, from childhood? Seeing how this job can really help you work through those things that you couldn't do with your parents as a child? What archetypes are you incorporating?

Worksheet 25: 'The Office' Archetypes

Name who is who in your office form the sitcom *The Office*. Include yourself.

Archetype	Greek Mythology	*The Office*	Who in your office represents this archetype
Hero	Apollo	Jim	This is you as the hero of your story. You're the sun, it's all about you. It is very important that we understand the archetype because there tends to be a narcissistic trend to this archetype. If it's all about us and we're the divine, what we're trying to do is obviously manage our fire in one direction or another, but we either play small, or we can scourge another in the process; neither is balanced. The shadow aspect of the sun is the darkness: what are you hiding behind your light? You're hiding the deadly sin or vices and afraid that someone will figure you out. List one thing you like and dislike about this person. Where do you display these same traits?
Caregiver	Artemis, Demeter	Phyllis	The caregiver is the moon and the mother archetype. The moon has to do with the mother, there's a very passive-aggressive codependent tendency. Like the moon changes its face every day, so does this archetype. You'll change your face to become whatever the other needs, so you can get your needs met. They put the needs of others before their own, but it isn't genuine. The shadow aspect of the caregiver is staying a child, and the belief that if I meet your needs, maybe my needs from childhood will finally be met. There's a lack of self-worth in this archetype and childhood wounding. List one thing you like and dislike about this person. Where do you display these same traits?

Archetype	Greek Mythology	*The Office*	Who in your office represents this archetype
Jester	Mercury, Hermes	Michael	The jester is Michael in *The Office*, the class clown or the office clown. They might be very good communicators and negotiators because it is Mercury in Greek mythology, the messenger of the gods. Yet they might also be the buffoon; they don't know the timing to make a joke or can't read the room and when it is not appropriate. The shadow side of this archetype is the need for validation and feeling intellectually inferior or superior. List one thing you like and dislike about this person. Where do you display these same traits?
Creator	Ares	Andy	The creator archetype has to do with competition and this person wants the next rung of the ladder, continuously. There's a big ambitious streak here and maybe we'll bulldoze those ahead of us to get ahead. In Greek mythology, it is Ares, and they tend to have a bit of a temper or anger issues. The shadow aspect is the unprocessed anger from childhood for having his boundaries repeatedly violated. If the creator can be competitive, physically strong and show anger, his boundaries won't be messed with again. List one thing you like and dislike about this person. Where do you display these same traits?

Archetype	Greek Mythology	The Office	Who in your office represents this archetype
Lover	Venus, Aphrodite	Kelly	The lover is Venus or Aphrodite in Greek mythology. In *The Office*, this archetype is represented by Kelly. Makeup, Instagram, the social butterfly at the low-consciousness level are her priorities. This archetype has a strong focus on relationships and wanting to be liked. Being heard in relationships and social interactions in the office is a critical theme of this archetype. The vanity of the lover archetype is the shadow aspect believing she is only worthy when her image is socially acceptable. Her self-worth is contingent on what others see. List one thing you like and dislike about this person. Where do you display these same traits?
Ruler	Lilith	Meredith	The ruler archetype is someone who has big ideas but it's to meet their own needs. They may cheat and love to party. This archetype can be vulgar, curse a lot at the low-level consciousness and create drama as a negative attention-seeking behavior. The shadow archetype is the prostitute, trying to be the seductress or scandalous so her low self-worth will never be on actual display. The scandalous behavior is to cover inadequacy and severe low self-esteem. List one thing you like and dislike about this person. Where do you display these same traits?

Archetype	Greek Mythology	*The Office*	Who in your office represents this archetype
Sage	Saturn, Cronus	Dwight	The sage is the Saturn or senex archetype from Greek mythology. They are the rule-keeper, the one that has the structure, that has to manage the office policies and procedures. They are the shadow archetype of the control freak. They're obsessed with details and procedures so they can control everything. The fear is being dispensable and found out that they don't contribute much because they're inadequate and easily replaced. List one thing you like and dislike about this person. Where do you display these same traits?
Rebel, Revolutionary	Uranus	Creed	The revolutionary in *The Office* is Creed. This archetype makes their own rules, always wants to be original, and they want to beat to their own drum. They get very caught up in ideals. In Greek mythology, it's Uranus. The shadow of the rebel is to create chaos and drama so that the real insignificance he feels is never noticed. They fail to have structure and plans and sell it as freedom. List one thing you like and dislike about this person. Where do you display these same traits?

Archetype	Greek Mythology	*The Office*	Who in your office represents this archetype
Innocent	Neptune, Poseidon	Stanley	We all have an innocent archetype, because we are trying to reclaim our child script, via a victim, from childhood. The innocent in the office tries to people-please, but the shadow is that they might avoid responsibility by playing small or playing childlike. The shadow aspects are victim, martyr, rescuer, and acting naïve so others take care of them while they manipulate with their covert power. List one thing you like and dislike about this person. Where do you display these same traits?
Magician	Pluto, Hades	Ryan	The magician is the loner archetype and tends to have a before and an after, as if two people. Ryan in *The Office* comes back to the office and he has two different roles. They tend to be visionaries and have big plans; however, they can create crisis and a lot of drama. They're always in in conflict, like a tortured soul. The shadow aspect of the magician is acting dark and unavailable because they were outcast as broken or demonic, when in reality they see the truth of things and rather than own it, they self-deprecate to feel they fit in with humanity. List one thing you like and dislike about this person. Where do you display these same traits?

Archetype	Greek Mythology	*The Office*	Who in your office represents this archetype
Everyman	Chiron	Angela	The every person archetype is also known as the commoner. They are often the wounded warrior or someone who wants to fix what's broken as a means to self-worth. He may be kind, empathic, and attached to his wound, but what really motivates them is being needed and being the good girl/boy. The shadow aspect is illness or OCD and needing to purify and clean everything. They don't feel there's anything special about them so the holier than thou attitude makes them feel superior to hide the inferiority. List one thing you like and dislike about this person. Where do you display these same traits?
Explorer	Jupiter, Zeus	Jan	The explorer is always ready to move. He doesn't really get hung up on things because he's always planning the "next thing." The shadow is the glutton and the escape artist. There's very little follow through and although they tend to have positions or power and appear wise, they're foolish and lack discernment. List one thing you like and dislike about this person. Where do you display these same traits?